U.S. Taxation of Partnerships

U.S. Taxation of Partnerships

Advanced Topics

Felix Lessambo

Wolters Kluwer

Published by:
Kluwer Law International B.V.
PO Box 316
2400 AH Alphen aan den Rijn
The Netherlands
E-mail: international-sales@wolterskluwer.com
Website: lrus.wolterskluwer.com

Sold and distributed by:
Wolters Kluwer Legal & Regulatory U.S.
7201 McKinney Circle
Frederick, MD 21704
United States of America
Email: customer.service@wolterskluwer.com

ISBN 978-94-035-3383-4

e-Book: ISBN 978-94-035-3384-1
web-PDF: ISBN 978-94-035-3385-8

Table of Contents

List of Abbreviations

AAR	Administrative Adjustment Request
AMT	Alternative Minimum Tax
BBA	Bipartisan Budget Act of 2015
BEAT	Base Erosion and Anti-abuse Tax
CFC	Controlled Foreign Company
COD	Cancellation of Debt
CPA	Centralized Partnership Audit
DI	Designated Individual
ECI	Effectively Connected Income
EPR	Entity Partnership Representative
ETF	Exchange-Traded Fund
FMV	Fair Market Value
FPA	Final Partnership Adjustment
FY	Fiscal Year
GAAP	Generally Accepted Accounting Principles
GAO	Government Accountability Office
IRC	Internal Revenue Code
IRS	Internal Revenue Service
IU	Imputed Underpayment
LLC	Limited Liability Company/Corporation
LLP	Limited Liability Partnership
LP	Limited Partnership
MLP	Master Limited Partnership
NAP	Notice of Administrative Proceeding

NASDAQ	National Association of Securities Dealers Automated Quotation
NFTL	Notice of Federal Tax Lien
NOPPA	Notice of Proposed Partnership Adjustment
NRA	Nonresident Alien
PIP	Partner's Interest in the Partnership
PPE	Plant, Property, and Equipment
PR	Partnership Representative
PTP	Publicly Traded Partnership
QDP	Qualified Derivative Payments
T.C.	Tax Court
TEFRA	Tax Equity and Fiscal Responsibility Act of 1982
TIN	Taxpayer Identification Number
TMP	Tax Matters Partner
Treasury	U.S. Department of Treasury

List of Figures

List of Tables

CHAPTER 1

Partnerships: A Business Organization Form

A partnership is an unincorporated organization with two or more members to carry on a trade, business, financial operation, or venture and divide its profits. There are different types of partnerships, including: (i) limited partnership (LP), which consists of at least one general partner and at least one limited partner. In an LP, the general partner is responsible for managing the company's day-to-day activities; (ii) limited liability partnership (LLP), which does not have a general partner, since every partner in an LLP is given the ability to take part in the management of the company; (iii) limited liability company (LLC), which is a hybrid business organization that mixes the best of corporations, partnerships, and sole proprietorships; and (iv) publicly traded partnership (PTP)

1.1 GENERAL

A partnership is an association of two or more persons ("partners") who come together to do business with the aim of making a profit and sharing it according to the partnership agreement. For tax purposes, a partnership is generally an unincorporated organization with two or more members that conducts a business and divides profits. Put differently, a partnership is an unincorporated organization with two or more members to carry on a trade, business, financial operation, or venture and divide its profits. However, a joint undertaking merely to share expenses is not a partnership.[1] Partnerships generally report their income on Form 1065, U.S. Return of Partnership Income.[2] Partnerships usually do not pay income taxes but pass—or allocate—the net income or losses to partners, who pay any applicable taxes. An unincorporated

1. For example, co-ownership of property maintained and rented or leased is not a partnership unless the co-owners provide services to the tenants.
2. GAO (September 2014)—Large Partnerships: Report to Congressional Requesters, p. 5.

organization with two or more members is generally classified as a partnership for federal tax purposes if its members carry on a trade, business, financial operation, or venture and divide its profits.

Example

(1) Wright and Donald are co-owners of a property inherited from their mother (Lucia).
(2) Wright maintained and rented or leased her co-ownership part to Maiden.

Task: Is there a partnership formed between Wright and Donald?
Answer: There is not a partnership unless the co-owners provide services to the tenants

Businesses have shifted from organizing as C corporations to partnerships and other pass-through entities in recent years. During tax years 2002 through 2011, the number of partnerships and S corporations of all sizes increased by 47% and 32%, respectively, while the number of C corporations decreased by 22%.[3] By 2017, we had 3,905,335 partnerships, 27,500,929 partners, with total assets of 32,403,619,868.[4]

3. IRS, "Partnership Returns: Selected Balance Sheet and Income Statement Items, Tax Years 1999-2011, Historical Table 11," Statistics of Income (SOI) Bulletin, *See* Figure 4. http://www.irs.gov/uac/SOI-Tax-Stats-Historical-Table-11 and IRS, "Returns of Active Corporations, Form 1120 and 1120S, Tax Years 2002-2011," Corporation Complete Book, http://www.irs.gov/uac/SOI-Tax-Stats-Corporation-Complete-Report. All estimates derived from samples have 95% confidence intervals that are within +/- 10 percentage points of the estimate itself, unless otherwise specified. Calculating percentage changes of numbers presented in above sources may not equal those we present due to rounding.
4. https://www.irs.gov/statistics/soi-tax-stats-partnership-statistics-by-sector-or-industry.

Figure 1.1 Partnerships by Number of Returns ($ Millions)

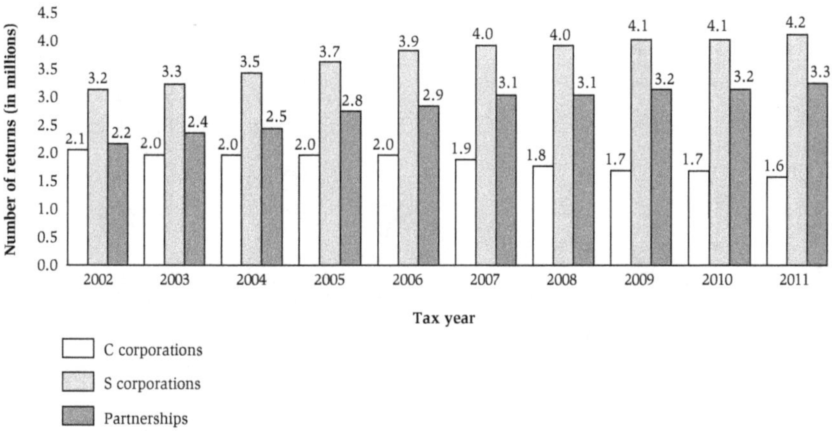

Source: GAO analysis of IRS data/GAO-14-732.
Note: C Corporations are generally taxed at the entity level under subchapter C of the Internal Revenue Code (IRC), whereas S corporations are corporations that meet certain requirements and elect to be taxed under subchapter S of the IRC, which provides that income and losses usually pass through to their shareholders.

The number of large partnerships has more than tripled. During tax years 2002 through 2011 (Figure 1.1), the number of large partnerships with 100 or more direct and indirect partners as well as $ 100 million or more in assets more than tripled to 10,099—an increase of 257%. Over the same period, the total assets of these large partnerships (without accounting for double counting) increased by 289% to almost $ 7.5[5] trillion.

5. GAO (September 2014)—Large Partnerships: Report to Congressional Requesters, p. 13.

Figure 1.2 Number of Partnerships and Direct/Indirect Partners

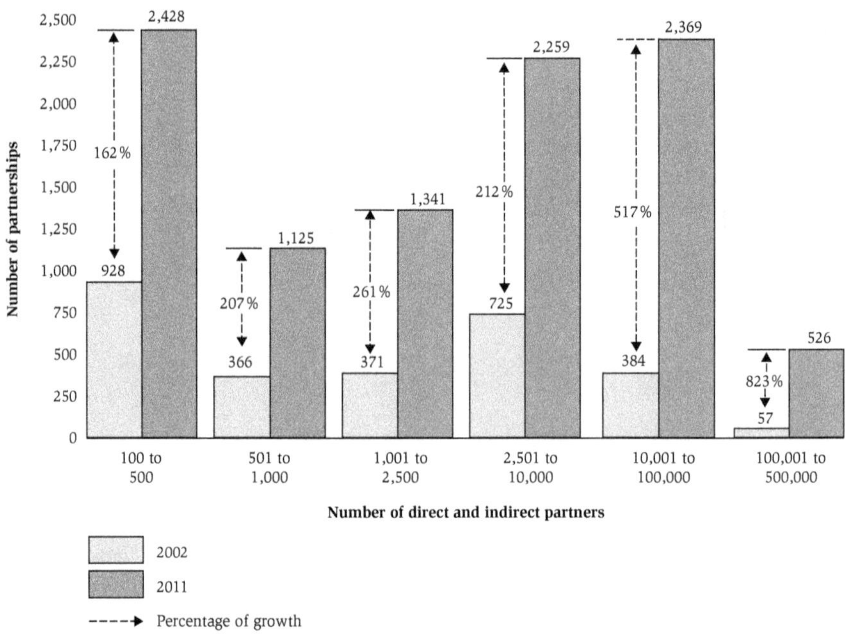

Source: GAO analysis of IRS data from Enhanced Large Partnership Indicator File and Business Returns Transaction File. Compliance Data Warehouse/GAO-14-732.

Most large partnerships have complex structures with thousands of partners and multiple tiers. Almost two-thirds of large partnerships had 1,000 or more direct and indirect partners in tax year 2011, but hundreds of large partnerships had more than 100,000 partners. Large partnerships with the most direct and indirect partners had the greatest increase from tax years 2002-2011 (Figure 1.2). The number of large partnerships varies considerably from year to year due in part to investment choices made by other large partnerships. An Internal Revenue Service (IRS) official said that the partnerships with more than a million partners increased from 17 in tax year 2011 to 1,809 in tax year 2012.

Figure 1.3 Number of Large Partnerships

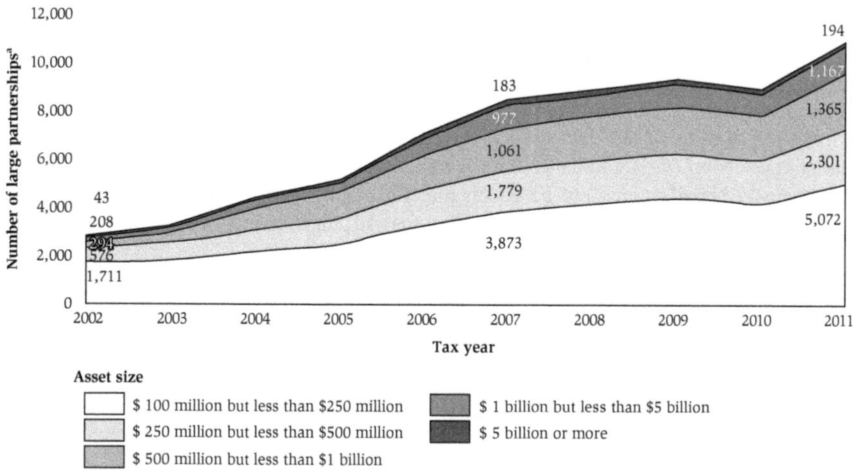

Source: GAO analysis of IRS data from Enhanced Large Partnership Indicator File and Business Returns Transaction File. Compliance Data Warehouse/GAO-14-732.

Large partnerships are concentrated in the finance sector (Figure 1.3). In tax year 2011, about 73% of large partnerships reported being in the finance and insurance sector, up from 64% in tax year 2002. About 87% of those in the finance and insurance sector in tax year 2011 engaged in financial investment activities, of which about 70% reported $ 1 billion or more in assets (Table 1.1).

Table 1.1 Large Partnerships per Sector of Activity

	Tax Year			
	Number		*Percentage*	
	2002	*2011*	*2002*	*2011*
Mining	18	170	1	2
Manufacturing	23	142	1	1
Transportation and Warehousing	43	114	2	1
Finance and Insurance	1,799	7,333	64	73
Real Estate, Rental, and Leasing	695	1,507	25	15
Professional, Scientific, and Technical Services	55	129	2	1
Holding Companies	56	233	2	2

	Tax Year			
	Number		*Percentage*	
	2002	*2011*	*2002*	*2011*
Other	143	471	5	5

Source: GAO analysis of IRS data from Enhanced Large Partnership Indicator File and Business Returns Transaction File. Compliance Data Warehouse. I GAO-14-732.
Note: Industry classifications are based on the North American Industry Classification System (NAICS). NAICS codes are self-reported by businesses and judgment may be needed to determine the most appropriate NAICS code.

1.2 TYPES OF PARTNERSHIPS

There are different types of partnerships, including the below.

1.2.1 Limited Partnership

A limited partnership (LP) is a type of partnership that consists of at least one general partner and at least one limited partner. In an LP, the general partner is responsible for managing the company's day-to-day activities. The limited partner in an LP does not participate in making managerial decisions for the business. In an LP, the limited partner is more like a silent partner that has invested in the business. In a limited liability partnership (LLP), all partners of the company are allowed to make management decisions for the company. In addition, general partners of an LP may be limited liability companies or corporations (LLCs), whereas LLCs and corporations may not be partners in an LLP.

When operating an LP, the general partner is liable for business losses and debts. This means the general partner may lose his personal assets because of losses and obligations that occur as a result of operating the business. Moreover, in an LP, the general partner must pay self-employment taxes on money received from the company, while limited partners are not required to pay self-employment taxes.

1.2.2 Limited Liability Partnership

A LLP does not have a general partner, since every partner in an LLP is given the ability to take part in the management of the company. An LLP is a form of partnership where all the partners enjoy limited liabilities. All partners are allowed to be involved in the management of the LLP.

1.2.3 Limited Liability Company

An LLC is an entity formed under state law by filing articles of organization as an LLC. Unlike a partnership, none of the members of an LLC is personally liable for its debts. An LLC may be classified for federal income tax purposes as either a partnership, a corporation, or an entity disregarded as an entity separate from its owner by applying the rules in Regulations section 301.7701-3.[6] An LLC is a hybrid business organization that mixes the best of corporations, partnerships, and sole proprietorships.

Each owner (also called a member) of an LLC has limited liability like a stockholder of a corporation. LLCs allow any entity, including individuals, partnerships, trusts, estates, corporations, or other LLCs, to be owners. They also offer greater flexibility than corporations—like no limits on the number of members—yet they have the tax advantages of a partnership, such as pass-through taxable income and losses. LLCs do not have to observe the formalities normally imposed upon corporations, such as producing annual reports, holding director meetings, and meeting shareholder's requirements. In addition, profit and loss can be allocated differently than ownership or partnership interests. Unlike corporations, which must distribute profits in proportion to each of the shareholder's ownership of shares, LLC members may distribute profits in any manner they want without regard to each member's capital contribution. Finally, with IRS "check-the-box" regulations, a business that is currently a sole proprietorship can change to an LLC with no federal tax consequences.

1.2.4 Publicly Traded Partnership

A publicly traded partnership (PTP) is an LP managed by two or more general partners that can be individuals, corporations or other partnerships, and that is capitalized by limited partners who provide capital but have no management role in the partnership. PTPs are also known as master LPs or MLPs.

IRS Definition

A PTP is any partnership an interest in which is regularly traded on an established securities market regardless of the number of its partners. This does not include a PTP treated as a corporation under section 7704 of the IRC.

SEC Definition

PTPs are business organizations that have two or more co-owners and are also traded on a public securities market such as the New York Stock Exchange (NYSE) or National Association of Securities Dealers Automated Quotation (NASDAQ). These co-owners can be individuals, other partnerships or corporations. A share in a PTP is referred to as a unit, and the shareholders are referred to as unit holders. When an investor decides to buy units in a PTP, he or she becomes a limited partner. A majority of PTPs engage

6. *See* Form 8832 and sec. 301.7701-3 of the regulations for more details.

in oil, gas and other energy-related businesses. Although investing in a PTP can seem very attractive due to its tax benefits, it can also create headaches due to reporting complexities and the uncertainty of future earnings.

Advantages

A PTP can, under specific circumstances, avoid corporate tax treatment.

To qualify as a PTP and avoid corporate taxation, 90 % or more of the PTP's gross income must consist of qualifying income (e.g., interest, dividends or royalties).

One of the largest advantages of investing in a PTP is that the partnership's income is subject to only one level of tax, at the investor level. The investor will receive a Schedule K-1 annually from the PTP allocating the investor's share of income, gains, deductions, losses and credits. At this point, the investor will then pay tax on the income received from the PTP at his or her tax rate. This is much more advantageous than investing in a publicly traded corporation, which is taxed at two different levels. Publicly traded corporations are taxed at the corporate level on profits and then once again at the shareholder level once dividends are distributed. Another advantage of investing in a PTP is the liquidity of owning a publicly traded stock. Whenever one sells his/her PTP units, the taxable gain is the difference between the sales price he/she has paid and his/her adjusted basis. Cash distributions decrease basis and are commonly disbursed quarterly.

Under the United States tax code, cash distributions are a return of capital and not taxed when received. If adjusted basis reaches zero, future cash distributions will be taxed as capital gains in the year received.

Disadvantages

An investor's initial basis is the price paid for the units and is then adjusted by the investor's share of income and deductions received. If PTP units are sold at a gain, there is a difference between taxing the gain at the preferential capital gain rate and the ordinary income rate. For these reasons, it is extremely important for investors to accurately track basis in their PTP investments. It should be noted that investment brokers rarely track shareholder's basis for PTP investments, but an adjusted basis will be shown on Schedule K-1 when all or some of the units are sold.

CHAPTER 2
Partnership Formation

> The partnership agreement includes the original agreement and any modifications. The modifications must be agreed to by all partners or adopted in any other manner provided by the partnership agreement. The agreement or modifications can be oral or written. Partners can modify the partnership agreement for a particular tax year after the close of the year but not later than the date for filing the partnership return for that year. This filing date does not include any extension of time. If the partnership agreement or any modification is silent on any matter, the provisions of local law are treated as part of the agreement. Partners contribute properties to the partnership at its inception. However, a contribution of money or other property to the partnership followed by a distribution of different property from the partnership to the partner is treated not as a contribution and distribution, but as a sale of property, if both of the following tests are met: (i) the distribution would not have been made but for the contribution; (ii) the partner's right to the distribution does not depend on the success of partnership operations.

2.1 GENERAL

A partnership[7] consists of two or more people, or other entities, who contribute money and property to start a business. A partnership, like an S corporation or an LLC, is a flow-through business entity, where profits and losses flow to the individual partners. The partnership itself is not a taxable entity, although it does have to file an informational tax return. Except for the members of LLCs and LLPs, each partner is personally liable for all debts of the partnership.

An organization formed after 1996 is classified as a partnership for federal tax purposes if it has two or more members and it is none of the following:

7. IRC §761.

- An organization formed under a federal or state law that refers to it as incorporated or as a corporation, body corporate, or body politic.
- An organization formed under a state law that refers to it as a joint-stock company or joint-stock association.
- An insurance company.
- Certain banks.
- An organization wholly owned by a state, local, or foreign government.
- An organization specifically required to be taxed as a corporation by the IRC (e.g., certain PTPs).
- Certain foreign organizations identified in section 301.7701-2(b)(8) of the regulations.
- A tax-exempt organization.
- A real estate investment trust.
- An organization classified as a trust under section 301.7701-4 of the regulations or otherwise subject to special treatment under the IRC.
- Any other organization that elects to be classified as a corporation by filing Form 8832.

2.2 "CHECK-THE-BOX" CLASSIFICATION AS A PARTNERSHIP

The Treasury Department's "check-the-box" regulations permit most unincorporated entities, such as general partnerships, LPs, LLPs, and LLCs, to be taxed as either a partnership (with two or more owners) or a C corporation.[8] Eligible entities make the election as to tax status by filing Form 8832 (Entity Classification Election). The "check-the-box" regulations are designed to provide eligible entities with a simple, certain means of choosing an entity for tax purposes. Entities with more than one owner can elect to be taxed as either a partnership or a corporation. An entity with only one owner can elect to be taxed as a corporation or a sole proprietorship. In the event of default (i.e., no election is made), entities with more than one owner are taxed as partnerships, and single-owner businesses are taxed as sole proprietorships. The election is not available to entities that are actually incorporated under state law or to entities that are required to be corporations under federal law (e.g., certain PTPs). Since organizations incorporated under state law will be taxed as corporations, entities that want to be taxed as partnerships but still want to have certain corporate characteristics will often organize as LLCs. However, there may be tax consequences for an entity that has been taxed as a corporation and elects different future tax treatment. For example, if an association previously taxed as a corporation elects to be taxed as a partnership, the election would be treated as a liquidation of the corporation, which could trigger taxable income to the corporation and its shareholders

8. Reg. §301.7701-1 to 301.7701-4, and 301.7701-7.

2.3 PARTNERSHIP AGREEMENT

The partnership agreement includes the original agreement and any modifications. The modifications must be agreed to by all partners or adopted in any other manner provided by the partnership agreement. The agreement or modifications can be oral or written. Partners can modify the partnership agreement for a particular tax year after the close of the year but not later than the date for filing the partnership return for that year. This filing date does not include any extension of time. If the partnership agreement or any modification is silent on any matter, the provisions of local law are treated as part of the agreement.

2.4 CONTRIBUTION TO A PARTNERSHIP

In general, a partner contributing any property to a partnership in exchange for partnership does not recognize gain or loss on the contribution. Likewise, a partner can acquire an interest in partnership capital or profits as compensation for services performed or to be performed without being subject to tax.

As a general rule, when a partner contributes a property to a partnership in exchange for a partnership interest, neither the partner nor the partnership recognizes a gain or loss. The rule is the same whether a partnership is being formed or is already operating. The partnership's holding period for the property includes the partner's holding period. The contribution of LP interests in one partnership for LP interests in another partnership qualifies as a tax-free contribution of property to the second partnership if the transaction is made for business purposes.

If a partner contributes property to a partnership, the partnership's basis for determining depreciation, depletion, gain, or loss for the property is the same as the partner's adjusted basis for the property when it was contributed, increased by any gain recognized by the partner at the time of contribution.

Example

Alpha and Omega formed an equal partnership. Alpha contributed $ 10,000 in cash to the partnership, and Omega contributed depreciable property with a fair market value (FMV) of $ 10,000 and an adjusted basis of $ 4,000. The partnership's basis for depreciation is limited to the adjusted basis of the property in Omega's hands, $ 4,000.

If the FMV of property at the time it is contributed is different from the partner's adjusted basis, the partnership must allocate among the partners any income, deduction, gain, or loss on the property in a manner that will account for the difference. The rule also applies to contributions of accounts payable and other accrued but unpaid items of a cash basis partner. The partnership can use different allocation methods for different items of contributed property. A single reasonable method must be consistently applied to each item, and the overall method or combination of methods must be reasonable.

Example

- Alpha purchased an undivided one-half interest in the depreciable property with her contribution of $ 10,000.
- Assuming that the depreciation rate is 10% a year under the General Depreciation System, she would have been entitled to a depreciation deduction of $ 500 per year, based on her interest in the partnership, if the adjusted basis of the property equaled its FMV when contributed.
- For the sake of simplification, let us assume that the depreciation deductions are determined without regard to any first-year depreciation conventions.
- Since the partnership is allowed only $ 400 per year of depreciation (10% of $ 4,000), no more than $ 400 can be allocated between the partners. The entire $ 400 must be allocated to Alpha.

If the partnership sells contributed property and recognizes gain or loss, built-in gain or loss is allocated to the contributing partner. If contributed property is subject to depreciation or other cost recovery, the allocation of deductions for these items takes into account built-in gain or loss on the property. However, the total depreciation, depletion, gain, or loss allocated to partners cannot be more than the depreciation or depletion allowable to the partnership or the gain or loss realized by the partnership.

2.4.1 Property Subject to a Liability

If property contributed to a partnership by a partner or distributed by the partnership to a partner is subject to a liability, the transferee is treated as having assumed the liability to the extent it does not exceed the FMV of the property.

2.4.2 Partner's Share of Recourse Liabilities

A partnership liability is a recourse liability to the extent that any partner or a related person has an economic risk of loss (EROL) for that liability. A partner's share of a recourse liability equals his or her EROL for that liability. A partner has an EROL if that partner or a related person would be obligated (whether by agreement or by law) to make a net payment to the creditor or a contribution to the partnership with respect to the liability if the partnership was constructively liquidated. A partner who is the creditor for a liability that would otherwise be a nonrecourse liability of the partnership has an EROL in that liability.

2.4.3 Disguised Sales

A contribution of money or other property to the partnership followed by a distribution of different property from the partnership to the partner is treated not as a contribution and distribution, but as a sale of property, if both of the following tests are met:

- The distribution would not have been made but for the contribution.
- The partner's right to the distribution does not depend on the success of partnership operations.

All facts and circumstances are considered in determining if the contribution and distribution are more properly characterized as a sale. However, if the contribution and distribution occur within two years of each other, the transfers are presumed to be a sale unless the facts clearly indicate that the transfers are not a sale. If the contribution and distribution occur more than two years apart, the transfers are presumed not to be a sale unless the facts clearly indicate that the transfers are a sale. A partner must attach Form 8275, Disclosure Statement (or other statement), to his or her return if the partner contributes property to a partnership and, within two years (before or after the contribution), the partnership transfers money or other consideration to the partner. For exceptions to this requirement,[9] a partnership must attach Form 8275 (or other statement) to its return if it distributes property to a partner and, within two years (before or after the distribution), the partner transfers money or other consideration to the partnership.

Form 8275 must include the following information:

- A caption identifying the statement as a disclosure under section 707 of the IRC.
- A description of the transferred property or money, including its value.
- A description of any relevant facts in determining if the transfers are properly viewed as a disguised sale.[10] *See* Regulations section 1.707-3(b)(2) for a description of the facts and circumstances considered in determining if the transfers are a disguised sale.

2.4.4 Contribution of Services

A partner can acquire an interest in partnership capital or profits as compensation for services performed or to be performed. A capital interest is an interest that would give the holder a share of the proceeds if the partnership's assets were sold at FMV and the proceeds were distributed in complete liquidation of the partnership. This determination generally is made at the time of receipt of the partnership interest. The FMV of such an interest received by a partner as compensation for services must generally be

9. *See* sec. 1.707-3(c)(2) of the regulations.
10. *See* Regulations sec. 1.707-3(b)(2) for a description of the facts and circumstances considered in determining if the transfers are a disguised sale.

included in the partner's gross income in the first tax year in which the partner can transfer the interest or the interest is not subject to a substantial risk of forfeiture. The capital interest transferred as compensation for services is subject to the rules for restricted property discussed under Employee Compensation in Publication 525, Taxable and Nontaxable Income. The FMV of an interest in partnership capital transferred to a partner as payment for services to the partnership constitutes a guaranteed payment, discussed under section 6.2 Guaranteed Payments.

A partner can acquire an interest in partnership capital or profits as compensation for services performed or to be performed.

Profits Interest

A profit interest is a partnership interest other than a capital interest. If a person receives a profit interest for providing services to, or for the benefit of, a partnership in a partner capacity or in anticipation of being a partner, the receipt of such an interest is not a taxable event for the partner or the partnership. However, the rule does not apply in the following situations:

- The profit interest relates to a substantially certain and predictable stream of income from partnership assets, such as income from high-quality debt securities or a high-quality net lease.
- Within two years of receipt, the partner disposes of the profit interest.
- The profit interest is an LP interest in a PTP.

A profit interest transferred as compensation for services is not subject to the rules for restricted property that apply to capital interests.

Basis of Partner's Interest

The basis of a partnership interest is the money plus the adjusted basis of any property the partner has contributed. If the partner must recognize gain as a result of the contribution, this gain is included in the basis of his or her interest. Any increase in a partner's individual liabilities because of an assumption of partnership liabilities is considered a contribution of money to the partnership by the partner.

2.4.5 Contribution to Partnership Treated as Investment Company

A partnership is generally treated as an investment company if over 80% of the value of its assets is held for investment and consists of certain readily marketable items. Gain is recognized when property is contributed (in exchange for an interest in the partnership) to a partnership that would be treated as an investment company if it were incorporated. These items include money, stocks and other equity interests in a corporation, and interests in regulated investment companies and real estate investment trusts.[11] For more information, *see* section 351(e)(1) of the IRC and the related regulations. Whether a partnership is treated as an investment company under this test is ordinarily determined immediately after the transfer of property. The rule applies to LPs and general partnerships, regardless of whether they are privately formed or publicly syndicated.

2.4.6 Contribution to Foreign Partnership

The IRS released final regulations (TD 9891) under IRC section 721(c) that continue to deny nonrecognition treatment to certain contributions of appreciated property by U.S. persons to partnerships with related foreign partners unless the partnership satisfies specific requirements. A domestic partnership that contributed property after August 5, 1997, to a foreign partnership in exchange for a partnership interest may have to file Form 8865, Return of U.S. Persons with respect to certain foreign partnerships, if either of the following applies:

- Immediately after the contribution, the partnership owned, directly, indirectly, or by attribution, at least a 10% interest in the foreign partnership.
- The FMV of the property contributed to the foreign partnership, when added to other contributions of property made to the partnership during the preceding 12-month period, is greater than $ 100,000.

2.5 DISGUISED SALES

A contribution of money or other property to the partnership followed by a distribution of different property from the partnership to the partner is treated not as a contribution and distribution but as a sale of property, if both of the following tests are met. (i) The distribution would not have been made but for the contribution. (ii) The partner's right to the distribution does not depend on the success of partnership operations. All facts and circumstances are considered in determining if the contribution and distribution are more properly characterized as a sale. However, if the contribution and distribution occur within two years of each other, the transfers are presumed to be a sale unless the facts clearly indicate that the transfers are not a sale. If the contribution and distribution occur more than two years apart, the transfers are presumed not to be a sale unless the facts clearly indicate that the transfers are a sale.

A partner must attach Form 8275, Disclosure Statement (or other statement), to his or her return if the partner contributes property to a partnership and, within two years (before or after the contribution), the partnership transfers money or other consideration to the partner. For exceptions to this requirement, *see* section 1.707-3(c)(2) of the regulations.

---

11. For more information, *see* sec. 351(e)(1) of the Internal Revenue Code and the related regulations.

A partnership must attach Form 8275 (or other statement) to its return if it distributes property to a partner, and, within two years (before or after the distribution), the partner transfers money or other consideration to the partnership. Form 8275 must include the following information:

- A caption identifying the statement as a disclosure under section 707 of the IRC.
- A description of the transferred property or money, including its value.
- A description of any relevant facts in determining if the transfers are properly viewed as a disguised sale. *See* Regulations section 1.707-3(b)(2) for a description of the facts and circumstances considered in determining if the transfers are a disguised sale.

2.6 DISTRIBUTION OF CONTRIBUTED PROPERTY TO ANOTHER PARTNER

If a partner contributes property to a partnership and the partnership distributes the property to another partner within seven years of the contribution, the contributing partner must recognize gain or loss on the distribution. The recognized gain or loss is the amount the contributing partner would have recognized if the property had been sold for its FMV when it was distributed. This amount is the difference between the property's basis and its FMV at the time of contribution. The character of the gain or loss will be the same as the character of the gain or loss that would have resulted if the partnership had sold the property to the distributee partner. Appropriate adjustments must be made to the adjusted basis of the contributing partner's partnership interest and to the adjusted basis of the property distributed to reflect the recognized gain or loss.

Disposition of Certain Contributed Property

The following rules determine the character of the partnership's gain or loss on a disposition of certain types of contributed property.

Unrealized Receivables

If the property was an unrealized receivable in the hands of the contributing partner, any gain or loss on its disposition by the partnership is ordinary income or loss. Unrealized receivables are receivables that have a value to the partnership, but for which the related income has not yet been realized or recognized under the partnership's method of accounting.

Inventory Items

If the property was an inventory item in the hands of the contributing partner, any gain or loss on its disposition by the partnership within five years after the contribution is ordinary income or loss. The term "inventory items" means: Property of the partnership of the kind described in section 1221(a)(1), or any other property of the partnership which, on sale or exchange by the partnership, would be considered property other than a capital asset and other than property described in section 1231, and any other property held by the partnership which, if held by the selling or distributee partner, would be considered property.

Capital Loss Property

If the property was a capital asset in the contributing partner's hands, any loss on its disposition by the partnership within five years after the contribution is a capital loss. The capital loss is limited to the amount by which the partner's adjusted basis for the property exceeded the property's FMV immediately before the contribution. If the disposition of any of the property listed in (1), (2), or (3) is a nonrecognition transaction, these rules apply when the recipient of the property disposes of any substituted basis property (other than certain corporate stock) resulting from the transaction.

2.7 BASIS OF PARTNER'S INTEREST

The basis of a partnership interest is the money plus the adjusted basis of any property the partner contributed. If the partner must recognize gain as a result of the contribution, this gain is included in the basis of his or her interest. Any increase in a partner's individual liabilities because of an assumption of partnership liabilities is considered a contribution of money to the partnership by the partner. If a partner acquires an interest in a partnership by gift, inheritance, or under any circumstance other than by a contribution of money or property to the partnership, the partner's basis must be determined using the basis rules described in Publication 551 concerning the basis of assets.[12]

Adjusted Basis

Increases

The basis of an interest in a partnership is increased or decreased by certain items. A partner's basis is *increased* by the following items:

- The partner's additional contributions to the partnership, including an increased share of, or assumption of, partnership liabilities.
- The partner's distributive share of taxable and nontaxable partnership income.
- The partner's distributive share of the excess of the deductions for depletion over the basis of the depletable property, unless the property is oil or gas wells whose basis has been allocated to partners.

12. Publication 551 (December 2018), Cat. No. 15094C.

Decreases

The partner's basis is *decreased* (but never below zero) by the following items:

- The money (including a decreased share of partnership liabilities or an assumption of the partner's individual liabilities by the partnership) and adjusted basis of property distributed to the partner by the partnership.
- The partner's distributive share of the partnership losses (including capital losses). The partner's distributive share of nondeductible partnership expenses that are not capital expenditures. This includes the partner's share of any section 179 expenses, even if the partner cannot deduct the entire amount on his or her individual income tax return.
- The partner's deduction for depletion for any partnership oil and gas wells, up to the proportionate share of the adjusted basis of the wells allocated to the partner.
- A partner's distributive share of foreign taxes paid or accrued by the partnership for tax years beginning after 2017.
- A partner's distributive share of the adjusted basis of a partnership's property donation to charity.
  Note. If the property's FMV exceeds its adjusted basis, a special rule provides that the basis limitation on partner losses does not apply to the extent of the partner's distributive share of the excess for tax years beginning after 2017. If contributed property is subject to a debt or if a partner's liabilities are assumed by the partnership, the basis of that partner's interest is reduced (but not below zero) by the liability assumed by the other partners. This partner must reduce his or her basis because the assumption of the liability is treated as a distribution of money to that partner. The other partners' assumption of the liability is treated as a contribution by them of money to the partnership.

Example 1

Ivan acquired a 20% interest in a partnership by contributing property that had an adjusted basis to him of \$ 8,000 and a \$ 4,000 mortgage. The partnership assumed payment of the mortgage.

Task: Determine the basis of Ivan's interest in the partnership
Answer: Adjusted basis of contributed property (\$ 8,000) – Part of mortgage assumed by other partners (80% (0.80) × \$ 4,000) (\$ 3,200) = Basis of Ivan's partnership interest (\$ 4,800)

Example 2

If, in Example 1, the contributed property had a \$ 12,000 mortgage, the basis of Ivan's partnership interest would be zero. The \$ 1,600 difference between the mortgage assumed by the other partners, $ 9,600 (80% × $ 12,000), and his basis of $ 8,000 would be treated as capital gain from the sale or exchange of a partnership interest. However, this gain would not increase the basis of his partnership interest. The adjusted basis of a partner's interest is determined without considering any amount shown in the partnership books as a capital, equity, or similar account.

Example 3

- Enzo contributes to his partnership property that has an adjusted basis of $ 400 and an FMV of $ 1,000.
- His partner contributes $ 1,000 cash.
- While each partner has increased his capital account by $ 1,000, which will be reflected in the partnership's books, the adjusted basis of Enzo's interest is only $ 400 and the adjusted basis of his partner's interest is $ 1,000.

The adjusted basis of a partner's partnership interest is ordinarily determined at the end of the partnership's tax year. However, if there has been a sale or exchange of all or part of the partner's interest or a liquidation of his or her entire interest in a partnership, the adjusted basis is determined on the date of sale, exchange, or liquidation. In certain cases, the adjusted basis of a partnership interest can be figured by using the partner's share of the adjusted basis of partnership property that would be distributed if the partnership terminated. This alternative rule can be used in either of the following situations:

- The circumstances are such that the partner cannot practicably apply the general basis rules.
- It is, in the opinion of the IRS, reasonable to conclude that the result produced will not vary substantially from the result under the general basis rules.

Adjustments may be necessary in figuring the adjusted basis of a partnership interest under the alternative rule. For instance, adjustments would be required to include in the partner's share of the adjusted basis of partnership property any significant discrepancies that resulted from contributed property, transfers of partnership interests, or distributions of property to the partners.

2.8 CASE LAW: COMMISSIONER V. CULBERTSON

The Supreme Court in Commissioner v. Culbertson[13] provided the foundation for determining when a partnership exists for federal tax purposes. The Supreme Court stated that a partnership exists for federal tax purposes under the following circumstances:

> considering all the facts—the agreement, the conduct of the parties in execution of its provisions, their statements, the testimony of disinterested persons, the relationship of the parties, their respective abilities and capital contributions, the actual control of income and the purposes for which it is used, and any other facts throwing light on their true intent—the parties in good faith and acting with a business purpose intend to join together in the present conduct of an enterprise.

13. The Supreme Court in Commissioner v. Culbertson, 337 U.S. 733, 69 S.Ct. 1210, 93 L.Ed. 1659 (1949).

CHAPTER 3
The Two Concepts of Partnership

For purposes of applying provisions of the Code not included in subchapter K, a partnership may be treated as an aggregate of its partners or as an entity distinct from its partners, depending on the purpose and scope of such provisions. The aggregate theory of partnership regards the partnership as merely the sum of the persons who comprise the partnership whereas the entity theory equates the group as similar to a corporation, a distinct and separate entity in and of itself. Conversely, the entity theory treats a partnership as a legal person, with existence and accountability separate from its owners.

3.1 GENERAL

Subchapter K of the Code is a blend of aggregate and entity treatment for partners and partnerships. The legislative history of subchapter K of the Code provides that, for purposes of interpreting Code provisions outside of that subchapter, a partnership may be treated as either an entity separate from its partners or an aggregate of its partners, depending on which characterization is more appropriate to carry out the purpose of the particular Code section under consideration.[14] That is, for purposes of applying provisions of the Code not included in subchapter K, a partnership may be treated as an aggregate of its partners or as an entity distinct from its partners, depending on the purpose and scope of such provisions.[15]

14. H.R. Conf. Rep. No. 2543, 83rd Cong. 2d. Sess. 59 (1954).
15. Rev. Rul. 89-85, 1989-2 C.B. 218, 219; *see* Casel v. Commissioner, 79 T.C. 424 (1982).

3.2 THE TWO CONCEPTS OF PARTNERSHIP

The general principle of law underlying aggregate or entity treatment of a partnership is set forth in the 1954 Conference Report on section 707,[16] which states the general proposition that aggregate or entity principles are applied as appropriate under the circumstances:

> Both the House provisions and the Senate amendment provide for the use of the "entity approach" in the treatment of the transactions between a partner and a partnership. However, that a partnership is to be considered as a separate entity for the purpose of applying other provisions of the internal revenue laws if the concept of the partnership as a collection of individuals is more appropriate for such provisions.

The existence of these two vastly different approaches often leads to confusion when there is no specific statutory language offering guidance. Congress is well aware of the confusion but seldom provides language to avoid it, presumably on the assumption that which theory applies depends on which is most appropriate for the particular section involved.[17]

3.2.1 The Aggregate Concept

The aggregate theory of partnership regards the partnership as merely the sum of the persons who comprise the partnership whereas the entity theory equates the group as similar to a corporation, a distinct and separate entity in and of itself. The aggregate theory is often used to ensure that income is correctly characterized as capital or ordinary and to allow limitations such as section 267 (related party loss disallowance) and section 170 (charitable contribution limitation) to be applied, while the entity approach is often applied in the interests of administrative simplicity and to ensure that certain rules are not abused. In the below-selected revenue rulings, private letter rulings, and Flexible Spending Account, the IRS has held that aggregate treatment of the partnership was most appropriate in the fact patterns examined:[18]

- Revenue Ruling 72-172, 1972-1 C.B. 265: A sale of all partnership interests, by a husband and wife, to a controlled entity was treated as a sale of the underlying assets of the partnership in applying section 1239. Thus, no-look through for IRC section 1231 or 1239.
- Revenue Ruling 89-108, 1989-2 C.B. 100: In this ruling, the Service held that income from the sale of a partnership interest may not be reported under the installment method to the extent it represents income attributable to the partnership's substantially appreciated inventory (within the meaning of §

16. H.R. Conf. Rep. No. 2543, 83rd Cong. 2d. Sess. 59 (1954).
17. Nellen and Karlinsky (1992), Section 1374 and the S Corporation (Fall 1992), Journal of S Corporation Taxation.
18. Monte A. Jackal (2017): Summaries of Aggregate and Entity Authorities, Tax Notes.

751(d)), which would not be eligible for the installment sale treatment if sold directly. The Service went on to expound:

> Because IRC section 751 effectively treats a partner as if the partner had sold an interest in the section 751 property of the partnership, the portion of the gain that is attributable to section 751 property is reportable under the installment method only to the extent that income realized on a direct sale of the section 751 property would be reportable under such method.

The ruling further stated that "the installment method is not available for reporting income realized on the sale of a partnership interest to the extent attributable to the substantially appreciated inventory which constitutes inventory within the meaning of section 453(b)(2)(B)."

- Revenue Ruling 90-112, 1990-2 C.B. 186: This ruling treated a partnership interest that is not itself U.S. property under section 956 as U.S. property to the extent that the partnership held U.S. property. The ruling adopted an aggregate approach to partnerships under section 956 as the Service was seeking to prevent a relatively easy end-around section 956 through the use of partnership entities. However, the IRS never explained in the ruling whether it was appropriate to apply section 956 by using the aggregate theory. Indeed, IRC section 956, and the regulations thereunder, did not provide the tax treatment of a controlled foreign company's (CFC's) investment in United States property through a partnership. Nonetheless, the Service argued that:

  > The purpose of section 956 of the Code would be frustrated if it were construed not to reach the United States property held by a CFC through a partnership. Thus, in the context of section 956, it is appropriate to apply the aggregate view of a partnership so that the United States property of the CFC includes United States property held by the CFC through a partnership. This result applies section 956 according to the substance of the arrangement, without regard to whether the form of the ownership is direct or indirect.

- Revenue Ruling 91-32, 1991-1 C.B. 107: In this ruling the IRS applied the aggregate theory on the sale by a nonresident alien (NRA) of a partnership interest not involving U.S. real property (and, thus, not subject to aggregate treatment under section 897(g)). The IRS held that foreign partners in partnerships operating in the U.S. (including foreign members of LLCs) are properly taxed on their capital gains under a look-through rule to the assets owned by the partnership. It is not exactly clear from the text of the ruling what authority the IRS relied on to reach this holding other than the acknowledgment that any other approach would prevent the IRS from collecting tax. The IRS flatly asserted that the rules for taxing partners on gains from the disposal of an interest in a partnership simply are different when the partner is not a U.S. person.
- Revenue Ruling 99-57, 1999-2 C.B. 678: The ruling addressed the tax consequences to a partnership and a corporate partner where the corporate partner

contributes its own stock to the partnership, and the partnership later exchanges the stock with a third party in a taxable transaction (or applying IRC section 1032 to partnership transaction). The IRS held that:

> Section 1032 is intended to prevent a corporation from recognizing gain or loss when dealing in its own stock. Under § 704(b) and 704(c), a corporate partner contributing its own stock generally will be allocated an amount of gain attributable to its stock that corresponds to its economic interest in the stock held by the partnership. Accordingly, the use of the aggregate theory of partnerships is appropriate in determining the application of § 1032 with respect to gain allocated to a corporate partner.

- Revenue Ruling 60-352, 1960-2 C.B. 208: In this ruling, the IRS held that the charitable transfer of a partnership interest where the partnership held section 453 installment obligations must be treated as a disposition of the underlying partnership assets in applying then section 453(d) (now section 453B). The ruling tackled the issue of income realization on contribution by a donor. In addition to a donation of encumbered appreciated property, certain other contributions may result in a realization of income by the donor. For instance, a donation of installment obligations was considered a disposition within (former) IRC section 453(d), allowing the donor to realize income. Tackling such an abuse, the IRS held that:

> Thus, while the partnership interest generally may be regarded as constituting a partner's interest in the profits and surplus of the partnership, the fundamental principles of Federal income taxation require that an interest in income earned by the partnership which has not been realized, or has not yet been subjected to taxation, be treated as distinct from any "partnership interest" which is recognized as a capital asset for income tax purposes. Therefore, unrealized or untaxed rights to partnership income may be transferred with, but not as a part of, the partnership interest which constitutes a capital asset.
>
> Based on the foregoing, it is held that a transfer of a limited partner's interest in a partnership appurtenant to which is a right to share in unrealized partnership income reflected in installment obligations receivable by the partnership constitutes a transfer of a capital asset coupled with a disposition of such installment obligations subject to the provisions of section 453(d) of the Code. To the extent that the transaction constitutes a disposition of installment obligations receivable, the gain is taxable to the transferor as ordinary income.

- Revenue Ruling 85-60, 1985-1 CB 187: In this ruling, the Service held that U.S. tax applied to a foreign beneficiary of foreign trust that happened to be a limited partner in partnership with U.S. permanent establishment. Relying on IRC section 702 (b), the Service argued that the character of distributive share determined at the partnership level to attribute a permanent establishment to a partner.
- Revenue Ruling 91-32, 1991-1 CB 107: In this ruling, the Service held that gain of foreign partner from disposition of an interest in a partnership with U.S.

permanent establishment subject to U.S. tax under applicable treaty based on foreign treaty resident's potential distributive share of unrealized gain of the partnership attributable to partnership's permanent establishment.
- Revenue Ruling 2004-3, 2004-1 CB 486: In this ruling, IRS held that service partnership's fixed base in U.S. was attributed to NRA partner who performed no services in the U.S. by application of §875(1) and the case law and revenue ruling applying that provision in the treaty context.

3.2.2 The Entity Concept

The entity theory is the concept of a business firm as a legal person, with existence and accountability separate from its owners. When individuals carry out a common enterprise as partners, a threshold legal question is whether the partnership is a legal entity. The common law said no. In other words, under the common law theory, a partnership was but a convenient name for an aggregate of individuals, and the rights and duties recognized and imposed by law are those of the individual partners. By contrast, the mercantile theory of the law merchant held that a partnership is a legal entity that can have rights and duties independent of those of its members.

The IRS has taken the entity approach to solving partnership questions involving the interplay of subchapter K and rules outside of subchapter K:[19]

- In Revenue Ruling 57-154, the IRS held that a taxpayer could not defer gain under the involuntary conversion rules of section 1033 by buying an interest in a partnership which owned property similar in service or use to the property converted. Thus, the IRS followed an entity approach by implying that the partnership interest is not viewed as proportionate ownership by the partner of each partnership asset. Similarly, under section 1031, partnership interests are not considered like-kind even if each partnership's underlying properties would be like-kind.
- In Revenue Ruling 75-62, 1975-1 C.B. 188, the IRS applied an entity approach for purposes of IRC section 805(b)(4), holding that a life insurance company should consider its investment in a partnership as an "other asset," rather than ownership of a proportionate share of each partnership asset. The Service stated:

  > There is no indication in the legislative history of section 805(b)(4)(B) of the Code suggesting that the adoption of the entity approach under the facts of the instant case is inappropriate, and in the absence of tax avoidance, there is no compelling reason to view the taxpayer's interest in the aggregate.

- In Revenue Ruling 87-51, 1987-1 C.B. 158, the sale of upper-tier interest in a partnership is not treated as a sale of the lower-tier partnership interest for

19. Monte A. Jackal (2017): Summaries of Aggregate and Entity Authorities, Tax Notes.

purposes of section 708(b)(1)(B) unless the upper-tier partnership is technically terminated on the sale. The entity theory of partnerships was applied because the IRS believed, without citation to any authority, that section 708(b)(1)(B) is an entity-oriented provision:

> Under the provisions of subchapter K of the Code, a partnership is considered for various purposes to be either an aggregate of its partners or an entity, transactionally independent of its partners. Generally, subchapter K adopts an entity approach with respect to transactions involving partnership interests ... Whether an aggregate or entity theory of partnerships should be applied to a particular Code section depends upon which theory is more appropriate to such section ... The termination of a partnership under section 708(b)(1)(B) depends on whether there was a sale or exchange of a partnership interest and on whether there was a transfer of at least 50 percent of the total interest in partnership capital and profits. *Because section 708(b)(1)(B) is an entity-oriented provision, an entity approach is more appropriate for that section.*

3.3 THE AGGREGATE AND ENTITY SPLIT IN THE COURTS

In the absence of any specific guidance by the IRS, courts remain split as to the partnership concept to apply in cases brought to their adjudication.

3.3.1 Entity Case Law

The courts, in a series of cases, have held that entity treatment of the partnership was most appropriate under the fact patterns examined in those cases.

Clinton Pollack v. Commissioner[20]

The Tax Court (T.C.) held that the sale of a partnership interest should be accorded capital loss treatment under IRC section 741 and not under IRC section 1221.

The facts of the case can be summarized as follows:

- H. Clinton Pollack, Jr., and Wendy Pollack were husband and wife who resided in Greenwich, Connecticut.
- H. Clinton Pollack, Jr., is a management consultant who was, during the years in question, associated full time with a large New York City consulting firm.
- In 1968, H. Clinton Pollack became acquainted with Leonard Turk, the designated general partner and formed an LP named Millworth Associates.
- The purpose of the LP was to invest in fledgling and troubled business concerns with the idea of developing such businesses into successful enterprises.

20. Clinton Pollack v. Commissioner, 69 T.C. 142 (1977).

- In August 1968, in anticipation of receiving a significant number of profitable consulting assignments, H. Clinton Pollack, Jr. borrowed $ 50,000 and became a limited partner in Millworth.
- The scheme of the partnership, as originally conceived—to provide its limited partners with professional assignments—did not eventuate.
- In December 1969, H. Clinton Pollack decided to withdraw from Millworth, since it failed to serve his purposes. As a result of the liquidation of his interest, he incurred a loss of $ 27,069.
- On his federal income tax return for 1969, H. Clinton Pollack claimed this amount as an ordinary business loss. Additionally, he filed an application for a tentative refund from the carryback of a net operating loss for 1969 of $ 15,743. Both deductions were subsequently disallowed by the IRS.
- The issue before the Court was to determine whether section 741, if applicable, or section 1221 was dispositive of the treatment accorded the gain or loss realized by a partner on the sale or exchange of a partnership interest.
- H. Clinton Pollack maintained that the interest involved failed to qualify as a capital asset under section 1221 and that, despite the language of section 741, the interest constituted an ordinary asset in his hands. Consequently, he concluded, the loss he suffered on its disposition entitles him to either an ordinary and necessary business expense deduction under section 162(a) or an ordinary business loss deduction under section 165(a).
- The Commissioner, on the other hand, contended that except for specific exceptions not relevant herein, section 741 mandates the loss be characterized as a capital loss.
- The T.C. agreed with the Commissioner that both the legislative history of section 741 and its language indicate that Congress intended it to operate independently of section 1221 so as to be dispositive of the character of H. Clinton Pollack's loss:

> In view of the foregoing legislative record and the plain language of the statute itself, we conclude that Congress intended section 741, if applicable, to provide capital gain or loss treatment on the sale or exchange of a partnership interest by a partner without regard to section 1221.

- Accordingly, the T.C. held that H. Clinton Pollack realized a capital loss on the disposition of his LP interest in Millworth Associates, irrespective of his motive in acquiring such interest.

Petroleum Corporation of Texas, Inc. v. U.S.[21]

- In *Petroleum Corp. of Texas*, the issue presented was whether a corporate partner in a partnership was subject to depreciation and depletion recapture under sections 1245, 1250 and 1254 upon its liquidating distributions to share.

21. Petroleum Corporation of Texas, Inc. v. U.S., 939 F.2d 1165 (5th Cir. 1991).

- While acknowledging that the transactions had a valid business purpose, the Commissioner argued that the aggregate theory of partnerships should be applied to protect the recapture provisions.
- The T.C. went beyond the written words to determine that the aggregate approach was most consistent with Congressional intent with respect to the particular IRC provision at issue. It held that depreciation recapture was required as if the corporation had distributed the partnership's assets to the shareholders, not that they had distributed a single asset, namely the partnership interest itself.
- The Fifth Circuit rejected the Commissioner's position, instead finding that the language of the statute was unambiguous and that, under the statute, partnership interests were not among the specific properties listed as being subject to recapture upon distribution.
- The Fifth Circuit *Petroleum* concluded that the aggregate theory could not be used to circumvent the clear language of the IRC:

> [T]here [is no] Code authority extant that would have authorized ignoring or "looking through" the partnership to conclude, fictitiously, that the corporations were distributing assets then held in partnership solution as distinguished from distributing interests in the partnerships themselves. Federal income tax law is replete with examples of applying the entity theory of partnerships on some occasions while applying the conduit or aggregate theory on others. It suffices that there is no authority for the government's expedient position that use of the conduit theory is authorized and that such use should somehow override the clear language of the Code.

Grecian Magnesite Mining, Industrial & Shipping Co. SA v. Commissioner[22]

The T.C. held that a non-U.S. person's capital gain from the sale of its interest in a partnership engaged in a U.S. trade or business generally is not subject to U.S. federal income tax, except to the extent attributable to the non-U.S. person's share of the partnership's U.S. real property interests.

The key facts of the case are as follows:

- Grecian Magnesite Mining, Industrial & Shipping Co., SA (GMM), a Greek corporation, invested in a Delaware LLC that was classified as a partnership for U.S. income tax purposes and engaged in a U.S. trade or business.
- In 2008, the LLC redeemed GMM's interest in exchange for cash. A portion of GMM's gain on the redemption was attributable to U.S. real property interests held by the LLC and taxable under section 897(g).
- A portion of the gain that GMM realized from the redemption of its partnership interest in Premier pertained to Premier's U.S. real property interests, and GMM conceded that this portion is subject to U.S. income tax. Still in dispute,

22. Grecian Magnesite Mining, Industrial & Shipping Co. SA v. Commissioner, 149 T.C. No. 3 (July 13, 2017).

however, was the remainder of the gain, which was not attributable to real property ("the disputed gain").
- The IRS, relying on Revenue Ruling 91-32, concluded that a non-U.S. partner's gain on the sale or taxable exchange of its partnership interest was effectively connected income (ECI) and subject to U.S. federal income tax to the extent attributable to property of the partnership that was used or held for use in the partnership's U.S. trade or business.
- The T.C. declined to follow Revenue Ruling 91-32, instead holding that GMM's disputed gain was gain from the sale of an indivisible capital asset (the entity approach) and thus was not subject to U.S. federal income tax.
- The Court stated:

> The parties agree that the transaction between GMM and Premier was a redemption. The payments GMM received in the liquidation of its partnership interest were, in the words of section 736(b)(1), made in exchange for the interest of such partner in partnership property, and therefore they are to be considered as a distribution by the partnership. The effect of such a distribution is governed by section 731(a), which provides: "In the case of a distribution by a partnership to a partner ... any gain or loss recognized under this subsection shall be considered as gain or loss from the sale or exchange of the partnership interest of the distributee partner."

That is, when a partner liquidates its partnership interest and is paid for its interest in the partnership's property, then under section 736(b)(1) the payment is considered as a distribution; and under section 731(a) the gain is considered to arise from the sale or exchange of the partnership interest, and not from the sale or exchange of the partner's portion of individual items of partnership property.

3.3.2 Aggregate Case Law

Conversely, courts, in a host of cases, have also held that aggregate treatment of the partnership was most appropriate under the fact patterns at issue in those cases.

Casel v. Commissioner, 79 T.C. 424 (1982)

The issue before the court was whether an aggregate or entity theory of partnerships was intended to be embodied in section 267(b)(2). The T.C. applied aggregate principles to invoke section 267 where a partnership accrued, but did not pay, management fees to a corporation controlled by one of the partners. The Court held that the related partner could not take a distributive share of the loss for this accrual even though section 267 did not, at that time, technically defer losses between a partnership and a corporation related to a partner of the partnership.

The relevant facts of the case can be summarized as follows:

- Edward Casel was a 50% partner in a partnership known as Edward Casel and Arthur Karpf, et al. The ownership of the remaining 50% of the partnership was divided equally among Arthur Karpf, Henry Karpf, and Robert Karpf, none of whom was related to Edward Casel.

- On August 1, 1973, the partnership purchased the Chelsea Towers Apartments, a rental apartment complex, from the U.S. Department of Housing and Urban Development, in exchange for a purchase-money mortgage in the amount of $ 2,340,000.
- On his 1974 and 1975 joint Federal income tax returns, Edward Casel claimed deductions of $ 8,915 and $ 8,649, respectively, as his distributive share of partnership losses attributable to the unpaid accrued management fees owed to Casel Agency, Inc.
- In the notice of deficiency, the Commissioner disallowed those claimed deductions.
- Edward Casel contended that the regulation was invalid because it treated the partnership as an aggregate of individuals for purposes of section 267, rather than a separate entity. The 1954 Code relied heavily, although not completely, on the entity theory of partnerships, and the inclusion of the term "partnership" within the definition of the term "person" in section 7701(a) seemed to negate the concept of a partnership as a collection of individuals.
- The Commissioner, on the other hand, maintained that section 1.267(b)-1(b)(1) and (2), Income Tax Regulations, was a valid regulation and, therefore, Edward Casel's 1974 and 1975 distributive share of his losses from the partnership must be reduced to the extent that such share includes the partnership's accrual of unpaid management fees to Casel Agency, Inc., a corporation related to Edward Casel within the meaning of section 267(b)(2).
- The T.C. found that since section 267 does not include members of a partnership and the partnership as related persons, transactions between partners and partnerships do not come within the scope of section 267. Such transactions are governed by section 707 for the purposes of which the partnership is considered to be an entity separate from the partners.

CHAPTER 4

Partnership Taxable Year and Accounting Methods

The taxable year of a partnership is determined as though the partnership were a taxpayer. Under IRC 706(b)(2)(ii) a partnership must conform its tax year to the tax year of its partners as defined under IRC section 706(b)(4). That is, if one or more partners having the same tax year own a majority interest (more than 50%) in partnership profits and capital, the partnership must use the tax year of those partners. A partnership accounting method includes not only its overall method of accounting but also the accounting treatment it uses for any material item. A partnership chooses an accounting method when it files its first tax return. Any subsequent change requires the IRS' approval.

4.1 GENERAL RULE

The taxable year of a partnership is determined as though the partnership were a taxpayer. Under IRC 706(b)(2)(ii) a partnership must conform its tax year to the tax year of its partners as defined under IRC section 706(b)(4). That is, if one or more partners having the same tax year own a majority interest (more than 50%) in partnership profits and capital, the partnership must use the tax year of those partners.

Example

- Azoumay, Brenda, and Connard formed a partnership ABC, LLP.
- Azoumay owns 60% of the capital and profit interest, while Brenda and Connard own 20% each of capital and profit interests.
- Azoumay's taxable year ends on June 30.
- Brenda's taxable year ends on April 30.
- Connard's taxable year ends on September 30.

Task: Determine ABC's taxable year

Answer: ABC's taxable year is June 30. The taxable year of Azoumay who owns 60% (more than 50%) of ABC capital and profit interest

If there is no majority interest tax year, the partnership must use the tax year of all its principal partners. A principal partner is one who has a 5% or more interest in the profits or capital of the partnership.

Example

- Bogucha LLP is a partnership created by four Fordham former MSA students: Azoumay, Brenda, Connard and Dindo.
- Azoumay and Brenda are calendar year partners, each with 40% of capital and profit interests.
- Connard and Dindo's calendar years end in June and September, respectively, with 20% of capital and profit interests, each.

Task: Determine Bogucha LLP's taxable year

Answer: Bogucha LLP's taxable year is the calendar corresponding with the taxable year of its two principal partners, Azoumay and Brenda, or December 31

If there is no majority interest tax year and the principal partners do not have the same tax year, the partnership generally must use a tax year that results in the least aggregate deferral of income to the partners. The tax year that results in the least aggregate deferral of income is determined as follows:

(1) Figure the number of months of deferral for each partner using one partner's tax year. Find the months of deferral by counting the months from the end of that tax year forward to the end of each other partner's tax year.
(2) Multiply each partner's months of deferral figured in step (1) by that partner's share of interest in the partnership profits for the year used in step (1).
(3) Add the amounts in step (2) to get the aggregate (total) deferral for the tax year used in step (1).
(4) Repeat steps (1) through (3) for each partner's tax year that is different from the other partners' years.

The partner's tax year that results in the lowest aggregate (total) number is the tax year that must be used by the partnership. If the calculation results in more than one tax year qualifying as the tax year with the least aggregate deferral, the partnership can choose any one of those tax years as its tax year. However, if one of the tax years that qualifies is the partnership's existing tax year, the partnership must retain that tax year.

The determination of the tax year under the least aggregate deferral rules is generally made at the beginning of the partnership's current tax year. However, the IRS can require the partnership to use another day or period that will more accurately reflect the ownership of the partnership. This could occur, for example, if a partnership interest was transferred for the purpose of qualifying for a particular tax year.

Example

A and B each have a 50% interest in partnership P, which uses a fiscal year (FY) ending June 30. A uses the calendar year and B uses a FY ending November 30. P must change its tax year to a FY ending November 30 because this results in the least aggregate deferral of income to the partners, as shown in the following table:

Year End 12/31	Year End	Profits Interest	Months of Deferral	Interest × Deferral
A	12/31	0.5	-0-	-0-
B	11/30	0.5	11	5.5
Total Deferral				5.5
Year End 11/30	Year End	Profits Interest	Months of Deferral	Interest × Deferral
A	12/31	0.5	1	0.5
B	11/30	0.5	-0-	-0-
Total Deferral				0.5

4.1.1 Exceptions

4.1.1.1 IRC Section 444 Election

A partnership can elect under IRC section 444 of the IRC to use a tax year other than its required tax year. However, certain restrictions apply to such an election. A partnership that makes a section 444 election must make certain required payments. Moreover, section 444 election does not apply to any partnership that establishes a business purpose for a different period.

To make a section 444 election, a partnership must meet all the following requirements:

- It is not a member of a tiered structure:[23] No election may be made under section 444(a) by an entity that is part of a tiered structure other than a tiered structure that consists entirely of partnerships and/or S corporations all of which have the same tax year. An election previously made will be terminated if an entity later becomes part of a tiered structure that is not allowed to make the election. A partnership is considered a member of a tiered structure if: (i) the partnership directly owns any portion of a deferral entity, or (ii) a deferral entity directly owns any portion of the partnership.
- It has not previously had a section 444 election in effect.
- It elects a year that meets the deferral period requirement.

If the partnership is adopting or changing to a tax year other than its required year, the deferral period is the number of months from the *end* of the new tax year to the *end* of the required tax year. The IRS will allow a section 444 election only if the deferral period of the new tax year is less than the shorter of: (i) three months, or (ii) the deferral period of the tax year being changed.

Example

- On January 1, 2016, Babel and Cico created B&C LLP.
- In the absence of an election, the *required* taxable year for B&C LLP would be a calendar year (12 months ended December 31).
- B&C made an election under IRC section 444 to use a FY with the FY ending September 30. The deferral period is 3 months (October 1 through December 31).

The section 444 election remains in effect until it is terminated. If the election is terminated, another section 444 election cannot be made for any tax year. Also, the election ends when any of the following applies to the partnership: (i) the entity changes to its required tax year; (ii) the entity liquidates; (iii) the entity becomes a member of a tiered structure; (iv) the IRS determines that the entity willfully failed to comply with the required payments or distributions.

4.1.1.2 52-53-Week Tax Year

A partnership can use a tax year other than its required tax year if it elects a 52-53-week tax year that ends with reference to either its required tax year or a tax year elected under section 444. A newly formed partnership can adopt a 52-53-week tax year ending with reference to either its required tax year or a tax year elected under section 444 without IRS approval. However, if the entity wishes to change to a 52-53-week tax year or change from a 52-53-week tax year that references a particular month to a

23. Defined in sec. 1.444-2T of the regulations.

non-52-53-week tax year that ends on the last day of that month, it must request IRS approval by filing Form 1128.

4.1.1.3 Business Purpose Tax Year

A partnership can establish the business purpose for a tax year by filing Form 1128. Rev. Proc. 2002-39 and Rev. Rul. 87-57 contain the IRS position on granting business-purpose FYs established by facts and circumstances. Apparently, obtaining a year that requires IRS approval will be very difficult. Rev. Proc. 2002-39 states that the IRS will grant a taxpayer permission to adopt, change, or retain a FY under the facts-and-circumstances test only in "rare and unusual circumstances."

4.2 PARTNERSHIP ACCOUNTING METHOD(S)

An accounting method is a set of rules used to determine when and how income and expenses are reported on in a tax return. A partnership accounting method includes not only its overall method of accounting but also the accounting treatment it uses for any material item. A partnership chooses an accounting method when it files its first tax return. Any subsequent change requires the IRS approval. A partnership can figure its taxable income under any of the following accounting methods.

4.2.1 Cash Method

Most partnerships use the cash method of accounting. However, a partnership with a corporation (other than an S corporation) as a partner, with average annual gross receipts for the three preceding tax years exceeding $ 25 million (indexed for inflation) cannot use the cash method, including any combination of methods that includes the cash method. Under the cash method, a partnership includes in its gross income all items of income it has actually or constructively received during the tax year. Income is constructively received when an amount is credited to the partnership account or made available to it without restriction. However, income is not constructively received if the partnership control of its receipt is subject to substantial restrictions or limitations.

Example

Broom is a calendar year taxpayer. Broom's bank credited, and made available, interest to his bank account in December 2018. Broom did not withdraw it or enter it into his books until 2019. Broom must include the amount in gross income for 2018, the year he constructively received the interest income. Broom cannot hold checks or postpone taking possession of similar property from one tax year to another to postpone paying tax on the income. Broom must report the income in the year the property is received or made available to you without restriction.

Under the cash method, expenses are deducted in the tax year in which the partnership actually pays them. This includes business expenses for a partnership contest liability. However, a partnership may not be able to deduct an expense paid in advance. Instead, it may be required to capitalize certain costs. Expenses paid in advance constitute another challenge to the deductibility rule aforementioned. An expense paid in advance is deductible only in the year to which it applies, unless the expense qualifies for the 12-month rule. Under the 12-month rule, a taxpayer is not required to capitalize amounts paid to create certain rights or benefits for the taxpayer that do not extend beyond the earlier of the following: (i) 12 months after the right or benefit begins, or (ii) the end of the tax year after the tax year in which payment is made.

Example

- *Cahn is* a calendar year taxpayer and pay \$ 3,000 in 2018 for a business insurance policy that is effective for 3 years (36 months), beginning on July 1, 2018.
- The general rule that an expense paid in advance is deductible only in the year to which it applies is applicable to this payment because the payment does not qualify for the 12-month rule.
- Therefore, only \$ 500 (6/36 × \$ 3,000) is deductible in 2018, \$ 1,000 (12/36 × \$ 3,000) is deductible in 2019, \$ 1,000 (12/36 × \$ 3,000) is deductible in 2020, and the remaining \$ 500 is deductible in 2021.

4.2.2 Accrual Method

Under an accrual method of accounting, a partnership reports income in the year it is earned and deduct or capitalize expenses in the year incurred. The purpose of an accrual method of accounting is to match income and expenses in the correct year. Income is generally included in gross income for the tax year in which all events that fix the partnership right to receive the income have occurred and the partnership can determine the amount with reasonable accuracy. However, the inclusion of certain income in gross income may be challenging. That is the case for:

(i) estimated income, and
(ii) advanced payment for sales.

A partnership can include a reasonably estimated amount in gross income and later determine the exact amount is different, and take the difference into account in the tax year you make that determination. Advance payments must be: includible in gross receipts under the method of accounting the partnership uses for tax purposes, and included in income in the partnership applicable financial statements (described in section 451(b)(1)).

Special rules apply to including income from advance payments on agreements for future sales or other dispositions of goods held primarily for sale to customers in the ordinary course of your trade or business. However, the rules do not apply to a payment (or part of a payment) for services that are not an integral part of the main activities covered under the agreement. An agreement includes a gift certificate that can be redeemed for goods. Amounts due and payable are considered received.

4.2.3 Change in Accounting Method

A change in a partnership accounting method includes a change not only in its overall system of accounting but also in the treatment of any material item. A material item is one that affects the proper time for inclusion of income or allowance of a deduction. Although an accounting method can exist without treating an item consistently, an accounting method is not established for that item, in most cases, unless the item is treated consistently. The following are examples of changes in accounting method that require IRS approval:

- A change from the cash method to an accrual method or vice versa.
- A change in the method or basis used to value inventory.
- A change in the depreciation or amortization method (except for certain permitted changes to the straight-line method).

However, approval is not required under the following situations:

- Correction of a math or posting error.
- Correction of an error in figuring tax liability (such as an error in figuring a credit).
- An adjustment of any item of income or deduction that does not involve the proper time for including it in income or deducting it.
- Certain adjustments in the useful life of a depreciable or amortizable asset.

CHAPTER 5
Partnership Anti-abuse Rules and the BEAT

Section 1.701-2(a) of the Income Tax Regulations provides that subchapter K is intended to permit taxpayers to conduct joint business (including investment) activities through a flexible economic arrangement without incurring an entity-level tax. Thus, there must be a bona fide partnership, and transactions should have a substantial business purpose. Partnership as a business entity has also been abused in tax sheltering. Because of its nature as a flow-through entity and its flexibility in allocating income among partners, the partnership form provides an attractive structure for tax shelters.

5.1 GENERAL

Subchapter K is intended to permit taxpayers to conduct joint business activities through a flexible economic arrangement without incurring an entity-level tax. Thus, there must be a bona fide partnership, and transactions should have a substantial business purpose. Unfortunately, the business structure has been used and abused by unscrupulous individuals and entities. Thus, it is no surprise that partnerships played a central role in the most recent generation of tax shelters: Enron, General Electric, Colgate-Palmolive, and many other corporations all used partnerships to structure abusive transactions during the last decade. In response to perceived abuses achieved by structuring transactions through partnerships, the Commissioner issued Proposed Treasury Regulation §1.701-2 on May 17, 1994. After considerable discussion, the final regulation was issued on December 29, 1994. The regulation is known as the partnership anti-abuse regulation.

5.2 THE ANTI-ABUSE REGULATIONS

Section 1.701-2(a) of the Income Tax Regulations provides that subchapter K is intended to permit taxpayers to conduct joint business (including investment) activities through a flexible economic arrangement without incurring an entity-level tax. If a partnership is formed or availed of in connection with a transaction with a principal purpose of substantially reducing the partners' aggregate federal tax liability in a manner that is inconsistent with the intent of subchapter K, the IRS can recast the transaction in order to correct the inconsistency. A transaction may be recast even though it falls within the literal words of a particular statutory or regulatory provision. The regulations identify three broad requirements as implicit in this intent:

1. The Substantial Business Purpose

Section 1.701-2(b) provides, in part, that if a partnership is formed or availed of in connection with a transaction a principal purpose of which is to reduce substantially the present value of the partners' aggregate federal tax liability in a manner that is inconsistent with the intent of subchapter K, the Commissioner can recast the transaction for federal tax purposes, as appropriate to achieve tax results that are consistent with the intent of subchapter K, in light of the applicable statutory and regulatory provisions and the pertinent facts and circumstances.

2. The Substance over Form Requirement

The form of each partnership transaction must be respected under substance over form principles. In most cases, the tax consequences must reflect the partners' economic agreement and clearly reflect a partner's income. Certain provisions under subchapter K, however, were adopted to promote administrative convenience (and other policy objectives) and may produce results that do not properly reflect income. Thus, an exception to the clear reflection of income standard is made for Code sections that clearly contemplate a result that is not a clear reflection of income.

3. The Proper Reflection of Income Requirement

Section 1.701-2(a)(3) provides, in part, that the tax consequences under subchapter K to each partner of partnership operations and transactions between the partner and the partnership must accurately reflect the partners' economic agreement and clearly reflect the partner's income. An exception to the proper reflection of income requirement is made in cases where the application of certain subchapter K provisions, adopted to promote administrative convenience and other policy objectives, produces tax results that do not clearly reflect the partner's income.

5.2.1 The Facts-and-Circumstances Approach

Under the Anti-abuse Regulations, each case must be determined based on all the facts and circumstances. Some, but not all, of the factors to consider are:

- The tax liability resulting from owning property through a partnership is substantially less than the tax liability that would have resulted if the assets were owned directly by the partners.
- The tax liability resulting from treating the transaction as a series of steps is substantially less than the tax liability that would have resulted if the steps had been considered as one transaction.
- Partner(s) have nominal interests, protection from loss, or preferred returns with little participation in profits.
- There are related partners.
- Allocations follow the literal language of Treasury Regulation §§ 1.704-1 and 1.704-2[24] but produce results that are inconsistent with the purpose of section 704(b) (particularly where one partner is exempt from U.S. tax).
- The contributing partner, or a related party, retains the benefits and burdens of the ownership of property that has been contributed to the partnership.
- Benefits and burdens of property ownership shift to a distributee partner, or a related party, before or after the actual distribution.

5.2.2 The Tucker Case

- The taxpayers entered into a series of highly complex foreign currency option investment transactions.
- Prima facie, all the transactions complied with a literal reading of the Code and generated more than $ 39 million losses deduction in FY 2000.
- The IRS disallowed the entire loss deduction and assessed a deficiency penalty. The taxpayers challenged the deficiency and the penalty. The IRS concluded that Tucker and his wife Laura jointly owed more than $ 15.5 million in taxes.
- The T.C. upheld the deficiency, finding that the taxpayers were not entitled to their claimed deduction because the underlying transaction creating the deduction lacked economic substance.
- The T.C. found that the transaction defied objective economic reality because the potential profit was *de minimis* compared to the expected tax benefit.
- The Tuckers appealed the T.C.'s decision on the basis that the T.C. erroneously applied the economic substance doctrine because the transaction complied with a literal reading of the Code.
- The Fifth Circuit upheld the IRS' stance that the underlying transactions lacked economic substance.
- The Circuit Court held that the economic substance doctrine allows courts to disregard transactions for federal income tax purposes if they have no effect

24. A partner's distributive share of any item or class of items of income, gain, loss, deduction, or credit of the partnership shall be determined by the partnership agreement, unless otherwise provided by sec. 704 and paragraphs (b) through (e) of this section.

other than on income tax loss, even if they formally comply with the U.S. Tax Code.

5.2.3 Abuse of Partnership as an Entity

Partnership as a business entity has also been abused in tax sheltering. Because of its nature as a flow-through entity and its flexibility in allocating income among partners, the partnership form provides an attractive structure for tax shelters. Individuals with substantial amounts of positive income from other sources, such as wages and salaries or self-employment earnings, could invest in partnerships and offset some (or even all) of that income with their distributive share of any tax losses from the partnership. Tax shelters are generally defined as "investments in which a significant portion of the investor's return is derived from the realization of tax saving with respect to other income, as well as the receipt of tax-favored (or, potentially, tax-exempt) income from the investment itself." Tax shelters commonly involve one or more of the following advantages:

- Deferral of tax liability through the use of tax provisions or tax preferences that accelerate deductions. Deferral, in effect, produces an interest free loan from the Government to the taxpayer.
- Conversion of ordinary income into capital gains or other forms of income subject to lower rates of tax.
- Leveraged purchasing which magnifies the other tax advantages.

5.3 PARTNERSHIP: BASE EROSION AND ANTI-ABUSE TAX

5.3.1 Base Erosion and Anti-abuse Tax

The Tax Cuts and Jobs Act of 2017 (the "Act") added new section 59A, which imposes a Base Erosion and Anti-abuse Tax (BEAT) on certain deductions paid or accrued to foreign-related parties. By taxing such payments, the BEAT "aims to level the playing field between U.S. and foreign-owned multinational corporations in an administrable way." A taxpayer that satisfies both the gross receipts test and the base erosion percentage test is referred to as an applicable taxpayer. A taxpayer is not an applicable taxpayer and thus does not have any BEAT liability, if its base erosion percentage is less than the base erosion threshold. The BEAT operates as a minimum tax, so an applicable taxpayer is only subject to additional tax under the BEAT if the tax at the BEAT rate multiplied by the taxpayer's modified taxable income exceeds the taxpayer's regular tax liability, reduced by certain credits. Because of this latter provision, the BEAT formula has the effect of imposing the BEAT on the amount of those tax credits.

5.3.2 Application of the BEAT to Partnerships

On September 1, 2020, the IRS released its final regulations which set forth operating rules for applying the BEAT to partnerships. In general, the final regulations provide that a partnership is treated as an aggregate of its partners and, accordingly, deem certain transactions to have occurred at the partner level for BEAT purposes even though they may be treated as having occurred at the partnership level for other tax purposes. However, the regulations provide an exception (the "ECI exception") whereby a base erosion payment does not result from amounts paid or accrued to a foreign-related party that are subject to tax as ECI. To qualify for the ECI exception, the taxpayer must receive a withholding certificate on which the foreign-related party claims an exemption from withholding under section 1441 or 1442 because the amounts are ECI. The 2019 final regulations do not set out specific rules for applying the ECI exception to transactions involving partnerships. The final regulations expand the ECI rules to apply to certain partnership transactions. The expanded ECI exception in §1.59A-3(b)(3)(iii)(C) applies if the exception in §1.59A-3(b)(3)(iii)(A) or (B) would have applied to the payment or accrual as characterized under §1.59A-7(b) and (c) for purposes of §59A (assuming any necessary withholding certificate were obtained).

> Example
>
> If a U.S. taxpayer purchases an interest in a partnership from a foreign-related party, then under the general BEAT partnership rules for transfers of a partnership interest, this transaction is treated as a transfer by the foreign-related party of a portion of the partnership assets to the U.S. taxpayer. *See* §1.59A-7(c)(3). To the extent that these partnership assets are used or held for use in connection with the conduct of a trade or business within the United States, this situation is similar to a situation where the foreign-related party directly holds the assets that produce ECI (e.g., in a U.S. branch). In that analogous situation, an acquisition of those assets by the U.S. taxpayer from which the foreign-related party is required to report ECI. The taxpayer may rely on the written statement unless it has reason to know or actual knowledge that the statement is incorrect.

The ECI exception reflected in §1.59A-3(b)(3)(iii)(C) may also apply in other situations, such as when:

(i) a U.S. taxpayer contributes cash and a foreign-related party of the U.S. taxpayer contributes depreciable property to the partnership;
(ii) a partnership with a partner that is a foreign-related party of the taxpayer partner engages in a transaction with the taxpayer; or
(iii) a partnership engages in a transaction with a foreign-related party of a partner in the partnership.

However, the general ECI exception reflected in §1.59A-3(b)(3)(iii)(A) would not apply if a U.S. person purchased depreciable or amortizable property from a foreign-related party and that property was not held in connection with a U.S. trade or business. Similarly, when a U.S. person is treated as purchasing the same depreciable or amortizable property from a foreign-related party under §1.59A-7(c)(3)(iii) because the foreign-related party contributes that property to a partnership, the ECI exception does not apply even though the property becomes a partnership asset after the transaction and the partnership uses the property in its U.S. trade or business.

To qualify for the aforementioned exception, the final regulations require a taxpayer to obtain a written statement from a foreign-related party that is comparable to a withholding certification provided under §1.59A-3(b)(3)(iii)(A), but which takes into account that the transaction is a deemed transaction under §1.59A-7(b) or (c) rather than a transaction for which the foreign-related party is required to report ECI. The taxpayer may rely on the written statement unless it has reason to know or actual knowledge that the statement is incorrect.

5.3.3 Treatment of Curative Allocations

Therefore, the final regulations retain §1.59A-7(c)(5)(v) along with an example that illustrates when curative allocations are treated as base erosion tax benefits; the final regulations also clarify that curative allocations that arise under section 704(c) as a result of a revaluation are treated in a similar manner.

5.3.4 Partnership Anti-abuse Rules: Derivatives Involving Partnerships

Section 1.59A-3(b)(3)(ii) provides an exception from base erosion payment status for qualified derivative payments (QDP). Section 1.59A-6(d)(1) defines a derivative for purposes of the QDP rules as a contract whose value is determined by reference to one or more of the following:

(1) any shares of stock in a corporation;
(2) any evidence of indebtedness;
(3) any actively traded commodity;
(4) any currency; or
(5) any rate, price, amount, index, formula, or algorithm.

The final regulations provide that the partnership anti-abuse rule for derivatives does not apply when a payment with respect to a derivative on a partnership asset qualifies for the QDP exception.

5.3.5 Anti-abuse Rules of §1.59A-9 for Basis Step-Up Transactions

IRC section 59A(d)(2) generally defines a base erosion payment to include an amount paid or accrued to a foreign-related party in connection with the acquisition of depreciable or amortizable property. However, §1.59A-3(b)(3)(viii) provides an exception to the definition of a base erosion payment for certain amounts transferred to or exchanged with a foreign-related party in a transaction described in sections 332, 351, 355, and 368 (the "specified non-recognition transaction exception").

The 2019 final regulations adopted a specific targeted anti-abuse rule in §1.59A-9(b)(4). That rule provides that if a transaction, plan, or arrangement has a principal purpose of increasing the adjusted basis of property that a taxpayer acquires in a specified nonrecognition transaction, the nonrecognition exception of §1.59A-3(b)(3)(viii)(A) will not apply to the nonrecognition transaction. Additionally, §1.59A-9(b)(4) contains an irrebuttable presumption that a transaction, plan, or arrangement between related parties that increases the adjusted basis of property within the six-month period before the taxpayer acquires the property in a specified nonrecognition transaction has a principal purpose of increasing the adjusted basis of property that a taxpayer acquires in a nonrecognition transaction.

The anti-abuse rule provides that when the rule applies, its effect is to turn off the application of the specified nonrecognition transaction exception only to the extent of the basis step-up amount. Moreover, IRC §1.59A-9(b)(4) states that the transaction, plan, or arrangement with a principal purpose of increasing the adjusted basis of property must also have a connection to the acquisition of the property by the taxpayer in a specified nonrecognition transaction.

CHAPTER 6

Transactions Between Partnership and Partners

For certain transactions between a partner and his or her partnership, the partner is treated as not being a member of the partnership. Guaranteed payments are those made by a partnership to a partner that are determined without regard to the partnership's income. A partnership treats guaranteed payments for services, or for the use of capital, as if they were made to a person who is not a partner. Special rules apply to a sale or exchange of property between a partnership and certain persons.

6.1 GENERAL

For certain transactions between a partner and his or her partnership, the partner is treated as not being a member of the partnership. These transactions include the following:

(1) Performing services for, or transferring property to, a partnership if:
   - there is a related allocation and distribution to a partner; and
   - the entire transaction, when viewed together, is properly characterized as occurring between the partnership and a partner not acting in the capacity of a partner.

(2) Transferring money or other property to a partnership if: (a) There is a related transfer of money or other property by the partnership to the contributing partner or another partner and (b) the transfers together are properly characterized as a sale or exchange of property. A partnership that uses an accrual method of accounting cannot deduct any business expense owed to a cash basis partner until the amount is paid. However, this rule does not apply to guaranteed payments made to a partner, which are generally deductible when accrued.

6.2 GUARANTEED PAYMENTS

Guaranteed payments are those made by a partnership to a partner that are determined without regard to the partnership's income. A partnership treats guaranteed payments for services, or for the use of capital, as if they were made to a person who is not a partner. This treatment is for purposes of determining gross income and deductible business expenses only. For other tax purposes, guaranteed payments are treated as a partner's distributive share of ordinary income. Guaranteed payments are not subject to income tax withholding. The partnership generally deducts guaranteed payments on Form 1065, line 10, as a business expense. They are also listed on Schedules K and K-1 of the partnership return. The individual partner reports guaranteed payments on Schedule E (Form 1040) as ordinary income, along with his or her distributive share of the partnership's other ordinary income. Guaranteed payments made to partners for organizing the partnership or syndicating interests in the partnership are capital expenses. Generally, organizational and syndication expenses are not deductible by the partnership. However, a partnership can elect to deduct a portion of its organizational expenses and amortize the remaining expenses (*see* business start-up and organizational costs in the Instructions for Form 1065). Organizational expenses (if the election is not made) and syndication expenses paid to partners must be reported on the partners' Schedules K-1 as guaranteed payments. If a partner is to receive a minimum payment from the partnership, the guaranteed payment is the amount by which the minimum payment is more than the partner's distributive share of the partnership income before taking into account the guaranteed payment.

Example

Under a partnership agreement, Divya is to receive 30% of the partnership income, but not less than $ 8,000. The partnership has a net income of $ 20,000. Divya's share, without regard to the minimum guarantee, is $ 6,000 (30% × $ 20,000). The guaranteed payment that can be deducted by the partnership is $ 2,000 ($ 8,000 – $ 6,000). Divya's income from the partnership is $ 8,000, and the remaining $ 12,000 of partnership income will be reported by the other partners in proportion to their shares under the partnership agreement. If the partnership's net income had been $ 30,000, there would have been no guaranteed payment since her share, without regard to the guarantee, would have been greater than the guarantee.

Including Payments in Partner's Income

Guaranteed payments are included in income in the partner's tax year in which the partnership's tax year ends.

Example 1

Under the terms of a partnership agreement, Erica is entitled to a fixed annual payment of $ 10,000 without regard to the income of the partnership. Her distributive share of the partnership income is 10%. The partnership has $ 50,000 of ordinary income after deducting the guaranteed payment. She must include ordinary income of $ 15,000 ($ 10,000 guaranteed payment + $ 5,000 ($ 50,000 × 10%) distributive share) on her individual income tax return for her tax year in which the partnership's tax year ends.

Example 2

Lamont is a calendar year taxpayer who is a partner in a partnership. The partnership uses a FY that ended January 31, 2018. Lamont received guaranteed payments from the partnership from February 1, 2017, until December 31, 2017. He must include these guaranteed payments in income for 2018 and report them on his 2018 income tax return. Payments resulting in loss: If guaranteed payments to a partner result in a partnership loss in which the partner shares, the partner must report the full amount of the guaranteed payments as ordinary income. The partner separately takes into account his or her distributive share of the partnership loss to the extent of the adjusted basis of the partner's partnership interest.

6.3 SALE OR EXCHANGE OF PROPERTY

Special rules apply to a sale or exchange of property between a partnership and certain persons.

Losses

Losses will not be allowed from a sale or exchange of property (other than an interest in the partnership) directly or indirectly between a partnership and a person whose direct or indirect interest in the capital or profits of the partnership is more than 50%. If the sale or exchange is between two partnerships in which the same persons directly or indirectly own more than 50% of the capital or profit interests in each partnership, no deduction of a loss is allowed. The basis of each partner's interest in the partnership (PIP) is decreased (but not below zero) by the partner's share of the disallowed loss. If the purchaser later sells the property, only the gain realized that is greater than the loss not allowed will be taxable. If any gain from the sale of the property is not recognized because of this rule, the basis of each PIP is increased by the partner's share of that gain.

Gains

Gains are treated as ordinary income in a sale or exchange of property directly or indirectly between a person and a partnership, or between two partnerships, if both of the following tests are met. (i) More than 50% of the capital or profit interest in the partnership(s) is directly or indirectly owned by the same person(s). (ii) The property in the hands of the transferee immediately after the transfer is not a capital asset. Property that is not a capital asset includes accounts receivable, inventory, stock-in-trade, and depreciable or real property used in a trade or business.

More Than 50% Ownership

To determine if there is more than 50% ownership in partnership capital or profits, the following rules apply:

(1) An interest directly or indirectly owned by, or for, a corporation, partnership, estate, or trust is considered to be owned proportionately by, or for, its shareholders, partners, or beneficiaries.
(2) An individual is considered to own the interest directly or indirectly owned by, or for, the individual's family. For this rule, "family" includes only brothers, sisters, half-brothers, half-sisters, spouses, ancestors, and lineal descendants.
(3) If a person is considered to own an interest using rule (1), that person (the "constructive owner") is treated as if actually owning that interest when rules (1) and (2) are applied. However, if a person is considered to own an interest using rule (2), that person is not treated as actually owning that interest in reapplying rule (2) to make another person the constructive owner.

Example

Individuals A and B and Trust T are equal partners in Partnership ABT. A's husband, AH, is the sole beneficiary of Trust T. Trust T's partnership interest will be attributed to AH only for the purpose of further attributing the interest to A. As a result, A is a more-than-50% partner. This means that any deduction for losses on transactions between her and ABT will not be allowed, and any gain from the property, in the hands of the transferee, is not a capital asset. Rather it is treated as an ordinary gain.

CHAPTER 7

Partnership Allocations

Under IRC section 704(b) and the regulations thereunder, allocations of a partnership's items of income, gain, loss, deduction, or credit provided for in the partnership agreement will be respected if the allocations have substantial economic effect. Allocations that fail to have substantial economic effect will be reallocated according to the partners' interests in the partnership. For allocations lacking substantive economic effect, the IRS will look to each PIP in determining allocations.

7.1 GENERAL

Partnership allocations are the division of the partnership's items of income, gain, loss, deduction, and credit between and among the partners. For allocations to be respected, they must have substantial economic effect. They will be respected if they are in accordance with the partners' interests in the partnership. Under IRC section 704(a) and (b), allocations of partnership income, gain, loss, deduction, or credit between or among the partners are generally respected so long as the allocations to each partner (1) are set forth in the partnership agreement and (2) have substantial economic effect.

7.2 THE PARTNERSHIP AGREEMENT

The partnership agreement includes the original agreement and any modifications. The modifications must be agreed to by all partners or adopted in any other manner provided by the partnership agreement. The agreement or modifications can be oral or written. Partners can modify the partnership agreement for a particular tax year after the close of the year but not later than the date for filing the partnership return for that year. This filing date does not include any extension of time. If the partnership agreement or any modification is silent on any matter, the provisions of local law are treated as part of the agreement.

7.3 THE SUBSTANTIAL ECONOMIC EFFECT

Under IRC section 704(b) and the regulations thereunder, allocations of a partnership's items of income, gain, loss, deduction, or credit provided for in the partnership agreement will be respected if the allocations have substantial economic effect. Allocations that fail to have substantial economic effect will be reallocated according to the partners' interests in the partnership. As a general rule, the economic effect of an allocation (or allocations) is substantial if there is a reasonable possibility that the allocation (or allocations) will substantially affect the dollar amounts to be received by the partners from the partnership, independent of tax consequences. That is, tax allocations in a partnership agreement will not be honored if they lack "substantial economic effect." Treasury has defined "substantial economic effect" in some of the most intricate regulations ever adopted. Much of the unintelligible legalese in partnership and operating agreements is designed to comply with these section 704 regulations.

7.3.1 The Economic Effect Test

In order for an allocation to have *economic effect*, it must be consistent with the underlying economic arrangement of the partners. The first economic test effect requires that there must be an "economic burden that corresponds to an allocation, or the partner to whom an allocation is made must ... bear such economic burden." The regulations under section 704(b) provide a safe harbor under which the IRS will respect a partnership's allocations as having economic effect. The requirements of the safe harbor are that the partnership must maintain the partners' capital accounts in accordance with section 704(b) capital accounting rules, that upon liquidation, the partnership must make liquidating distributions in accordance with the partners' positive capital account balances, and that a partner is unconditionally obligated to restore a deficit capital account balance following a liquidation of the partner's partnership interest.

Capital Account Maintenance

IRC section 704(b) requires that a partnership asset be recorded at FMV rather than at cost basis. This can often prove difficult when the partners are contributing assets other than cash or marketable securities to the partnership. The Treasury regulations provide that the FMV of the property contributed to the partnership is determined using an arm's length standard where the parties have adverse interests.

Partners' capital accounts are equity accounts kept in the accounting records of a partnership. Capital accounts are adjusted upward or downward each year depending on the transactions that occurred within the partnership. The goal of a capital account is to track a partner's economic investment in the partnership.

A partner's capital account initially consists of their initial capital contributions (cash + FMV) of property, net of liabilities associated with the property).

Each partner's capital account is *increased* by the following:

- Additional cash contributed to the partnership by the partner.
- The FMV of additional property contributed by the partner, net of liabilities associated with the property.
- Allocations of partnership income to the partner (both taxable and tax-exempt income).
- Positive 704(b) revaluations (book-up adjustments).

Each partner's capital account is *decreased* by the following:

- Allocations of partnership losses to the partner (both tax-deductible losses and nondeductible expenses).
- The FMV of property distributed to the partner.

Note: a distribution of property triggers book gain or loss that then increases or decreases the partners' capital accounts; then the partners' capital accounts are reduced by their pro rata share of the FMV of the distributed property:

- The amount of any cash distributed to the partner.
- Negative 704(b) revaluations (book-down adjustments).
- A Positive Capital Account Balance.

Upon liquidation, the partnership must make liquidating distributions in accordance with the partners' positive capital account balances, and a partner is unconditionally obligated to restore a deficit capital account balance following a liquidation of the partner's partnership interest.

Reevaluation of the Capital Account

In addition, the capital account maintenance rules permit a partnership to revalue its assets and restate the partners' capital accounts to reflect each partner's economic share of the underlying assets at FMV, but only if the adjustments are made principally for a substantial nontax business purpose in connection with specific events. These events are commonly referred to as "revaluation events." Regulations section 1.704-1(b)(2)(iv)(f) permits a partnership to revalue its property in connection with: (1) contributions of money or property by a new or existing partner in exchange for a partnership interest; (2) distributions of money or property to a partner as consideration for a partnership interest; (3) the grant of a partnership interest in exchange for services; (4) the issuance of a non-compensatory option; and (5) under Generally Accepted Accounting Principles (GAAP), if the partnership is a securities partnership (substantially all the assets of which are readily traded on an established securities market).

Example

- Ms. Bogus, a new partner contributes $ 20,000 for a one-third interest in AC Partnership (AC LLP).
- Assuming that Ms. Bogus is not related to the two other partners, and the parties are dealing at arm's length.

Task: Re-evaluate the assets of AC LLP

Answer: the partnership assets should have an FMV of $ 60,000 immediately after the contribution, and it can be inferred that the assets had an FMV of $ 40,000 immediately before Ms. Bogus joined

7.3.2 The Substantiality Test

The economic effect of an allocation (or allocations) is substantial if there is a reasonable possibility that the allocation (or allocations) will substantially affect the dollar amounts to be received by the partners from the partnership, independent of tax consequences.

7.4 PARTNER'S INTEREST IN THE PARTNERSHIP

For allocations lacking substantive economic effect, the IRS will look to each PIP in determining allocations:

- PIP is intended to signify the manner in which the partners have agreed to share the economic benefit or burden (if any) corresponding to the income, gain, loss, deduction or credit (or item thereof) that is allocated.
- It is determined by taking into account all facts and circumstances relating to the economic arrangement of the partners.
- Factors include: (a) partners' relative contributions; (b) partners' interests in economic profits and losses (if different than that in taxable income or loss); (c) partners' interests in cash flow and other non-liquidating distributions; and (d) partners' rights to distributions of capital upon liquidation.
- There is very little guidance as to how the IRS will weigh the various factors in determining PIP.

7.5 IRC SECTION 704(C) ALLOCATIONS

IRC section 704(c) aims to prevent a partner from contributing appreciated property to a partnership and then shifting that pre-contribution gain to non-contributing partner(s).

Example 1

- Azoumay and Brenda formed AB LLP.
- Azoumay contributes a Plant, Property, and Equipment (PPE) with a tax basis of $ 6,000 and an FMV of $ 15,000.
- Brenda contributes $ 15,000 in cash.
- Azoumay and Brenda share all income and loss 50/50.

Azoumay		*Brenda*	
Capital account	Tax basis	Capital account	Tax basis
$ 15,000	$ 6,000	$ 15,000	$ 15,000

NB: Upon formation, IRC section 721 provides that no gain/loss shall be recognized when Azoumay transfers the PPE to AB LLP. Rather, the g/l, if any, is deferred by virtue of IRC sections 722 and 723.

Example 2

- Same fact as under Example 1 save that AB LLP sold the PPE for $ 15,000 and recognized a capital gain of ($ 15,000-$ 6,000) of $ 9,000.

Task: How shall Azoumay and Brenda split the capital gain?

Answer: In the absence of IRC section 704, Azoumay and Brenda shall split the gain 50/50. That is, (i) tax gain = $ 15,000–$ 6,000 = $ 9,000; and (ii) book gain: $ 15,000-$ 15,000 = 0

	Azoumay		*Brenda*		*AB LLP*	
	Capital account	*Tax basis*	*Capital account*	*Tax basis*	*Capital account*	*Tax basis*
Initial contribution	$ 15,000	$ 6,000	$ 15,000	$ 15,000	$ 30,000	$ 21,000
Gain on sale of PPE	$ 0	$ 4,500	$ 0	$ 4,500	$ 0	$ 9,000
Total	$ 15,000	$ 10,500	$ 15,000	$ 19,500	$ 30,000	$ 30,000

NB: Though the disconnect between book and capital account can eventually be reconciled upon liquidation, it creates issues from the timing and the character (short term or long term) of the capital gain or loss.

Example 3

- Same facts as in Examples 1 and 2.
- Assume now that AB LLP liquidates and distributes $ 80,000 it held in cash.

Task: Distribute the liquidating proceeds between Azoumay and Brenda

Answer: Upon liquidating-distribution: (i) Azoumay recognizes a capital gain of ($ 15,000-$ 10,500) = $ 4,500 and (ii) Brenda recognizes a capital loss of ($ 15,000-$ 19,500) = $ 4,500

IRC section 704(c) applies in situations where a contributed property has an FMV different from its basis, or when a reevaluating event such as the admission of a new partner occurs. Thus, the purpose of section 704(c) is to prevent taxable gain or loss inherent in property at time of contribution from being shifted to another partner. IRC section704(c)(1)(C) provides special rules for contributions of property with built-in losses intended to prevent any shifting of the benefit of the tax basis in excess of value to another partner. IRC section 704(c)(1)(C) applies to actual contributions and therefore impacts forward section 704(c) allocations. Section 704(c) tax allocations are determined after section 704(b) book allocations are determined. The Regulations thereunder provide three generally acceptable methods:

7.5.1 The Traditional Method

The operative rule under the traditional method is that "Tax follows Book." That is, the non-contributing partner receives tax allocations equal to its share of book items, and the contributing partner receives residual tax allocations. There is an exception known as the "ceiling limitation" which stipulated that in situations where the total income, gain, loss or deduction allocated to non-contributing partners with respect to contributed property does not exceed the total partnership income, gain, loss or deduction recognized by partnership with respect to that property for the taxable year, a portion of the built-in gain or loss, the non-contributing partners may not receive tax allocations equal to their share of book items. Put differently, the traditional method allocates tax items to the non-contributing partner(s) to attempt to match "book" allocation; if insufficient tax items, then "ceiling rule" prevents further allocations. The traditional method follows five steps: (i) computation of the tax item; (ii) computation of the book item; (iii) allocation of the book item; (iv) allocation of the tax item to the non-contributing partner to the extent of its share of the book item; and (v) allocation of the residual tax item, if any, to the contributing partner.

Example Operation of the Traditional Method

(i) Calculation of built-in gain on contribution:
- A and B form partnership AB and agree that each will be allocated a 50% share of all partnership items and that AB will make allocations under section 704(c) using the traditional method under paragraph (b) of this section.
- A contributes depreciable property with an adjusted tax basis of $ 4,000 and a book value of $ 10,000, and B contributes $ 10,000 cash.
- Under paragraph (a)(3) of this section, A has a built-in gain of $ 6,000, the excess of the partnership's book value for the property ($ 10,000) over A's adjusted tax basis in the property at the time of contribution ($ 4,000).

(ii) Allocation of tax depreciation:
- The property is depreciated using the straight-line method over a 10-year recovery period. Because the property depreciates at an annual rate of 10%, B would have been entitled to a depreciation deduction of $ 500 per year for both book and tax purposes if the adjusted tax basis of the property equaled its FMV at the time of contribution.
- Although each partner is allocated $ 500 of book depreciation per year, the partnership is allowed a tax depreciation deduction of only $ 400 per year (10% of $ 4,000).
- The partnership can allocate only $ 400 of tax depreciation under the ceiling rule of paragraph (b)(1) of this section, and it must be allocated entirely to B.
- In AB's first year, the proceeds generated by the equipment exactly equal AB's operating expenses.
- At the end of that year, the book value of the property is $ 9,000 ($ 10,000 minus the $ 1,000 book depreciation deduction), and the adjusted tax basis is $ 3,600 ($ 4,000 minus the $ 400 tax depreciation deduction).
- A's built-in gain with respect to the property decreases to $ 5,400 ($ 9,000 book value minus $ 3,600 adjusted tax basis).
- Also, at the end of AB's first year, A has a $ 9,500 book capital account and a $ 4,000 tax basis in A's partnership interest.
- B has a $ 9,500 book capital account and a $ 9,600 adjusted tax basis in B's partnership interest.

(iii) Sale of the property:
- If AB sells the property at the beginning of AB's second year for $ 9,000, AB realizes a tax gain of $ 5,400 ($ 9,000, the amount realized, minus the adjusted tax basis of $ 3,600).
- Under paragraph (b)(1) of this section, the entire $ 5,400 gain must be allocated to A because the property A contributed has that much built-in gain remaining.

- If AB sells the property at the beginning of AB's second year for $ 10,000, AB realizes tax gain of $ 6,400 ($ 10,000, the amount realized, minus the adjusted tax basis of $ 3,600).
- Under paragraph (b)(1) of this section, only $ 5,400 of gain must be allocated to A to account for A's built-in gain. The remaining $ 1,000 of gain is allocated equally between A and B in accordance with the partnership agreement.
- If AB sells the property for less than the $ 9,000 book value, AB realizes a tax gain of less than $ 5,400, and the entire gain must be allocated to A.

(iv) Termination and liquidation of partnership:

- If AB sells the property at the beginning of AB's second year for $ 9,000, and AB engages in no other transactions that year, A will recognize a gain of $ 5,400, and B will recognize no income or loss.
- A's adjusted tax basis for A's interest in AB will then be $ 9,400 ($ 4,000, A's original tax basis, increased by the gain of $ 5,400).
- B's adjusted tax basis for B's interest in AB will be $ 9,600 ($ 10,000, B's original tax basis, minus the $ 400 depreciation deduction in the first partnership year).
- If the partnership then terminates and distributes its assets ($ 19,000 in cash) to A and B in proportion to their capital account balances, A will recognize a capital gain of $ 100 ($ 9,500, the amount distributed to A, minus $ 9,400, the adjusted tax basis of A's interest). B will recognize a capital loss of $ 100 (the excess of B's adjusted tax basis, $ 9,600, over the amount received, $ 9,500).

7.5.2 Traditional Method with Curatives

The traditional method with curatives is designed to help correct the distortions created by the ceiling rule. Thus, a partnership may make reasonable curative allocations to reduce or eliminate disparities between book and tax items of non-contributing partners. The traditional method with curatives allocates items of like character from contributing partner to non-contributing partner(s) to offset the impact of the ceiling rule; complete offset can be accomplished only if there are sufficient items of like character and all parties agree to such an allocation. Like the traditional method, the traditional method with curatives also follows a five-step approach, except that tax items (gain/ loss/ depreciation) from other properties are used to make up for some or all ceiling rule distortions in step four. Finally, the curative allocations must be *reasonable* in amount, timing, and type. As to the amount, curative allocation cannot exceed the ceiling distortion for that FY (or prior years if cure is for ceiling limitation on disposition). As to the timing, a curative allocation can offset the ceiling distortions for prior years if the allocation is made over economic life of the property and the allocation is provided in partnership agreement at the time of the contribution. Last, as to the type, a curative allocation must be expected to have substantially the same effect on each partner's tax liability as the tax item is limited by the ceiling rule. Expectation is generally tested at the time the property is contributed and the curative allocation is made part of the partnership agreement.

Example 1

	E		*F*	
Items	*Book*	*Tax*	*Book*	*Tax*
Initial Contribution	$ 10,000	$ 4,000	$ 10,000	$ 10,000
Depreciation	(500)	(0)	(500)	(400)
Sales Income	350	350	350	350
	$ 9,850	$ 4,350	$ 9,850	$ 9,950

Example 2

	E		*F*	
Items	*Book*	*Tax*	*Book*	*Tax*
Initial Contribution	$ 10,000	$ 4,000	$ 10,000	$ 10,000
Depreciation	(500)	(0)	(500)	(400)
Sales Income	350	450	350	250
	$ 9,850	$ 4,450	$ 9,850	$ 9,850

Example 1 Reasonable and Unreasonable Curative Allocations

Facts

- E and F form partnership EF and agree that each will be allocated a 50% share of all partnership items and that EF will make allocations under section 704(c) using the traditional method with curative allocations under paragraph (c) of this section.
- E contributes equipment with an adjusted tax basis of $ 4,000 and a book value of $ 10,000. The equipment has 10 years remaining on its cost recovery schedule and is depreciable using the straight-line method.
- At the time of contribution, E has a built-in gain of $ 6,000, and therefore, the equipment is section 704(c) property.
- F contributes $ 10,000 of cash, which EF uses to buy inventory for resale. In EF's first year, the revenue generated by the equipment equals EF's operating

expenses. The equipment generates $ 1,000 of book depreciation and $ 400 of tax depreciation for each of 10 years.

- At the end of the first year EF sells all the inventory for $ 10,700, recognizing $ 700 of income. The partners anticipate that the inventory income will have substantially the same effect on their tax liabilities as income from E's contributed equipment.
- Under the traditional method of paragraph (b) of this section, E and F would each be allocated $ 350 of income from the sale of inventory for book and tax purposes and $ 500 of depreciation for book purposes. The $ 400 of tax depreciation would all be allocated to F.

- Thus, at the end of the first year, E and F's book and tax capital accounts would be as follows:

	E		F	
Items	*Book*	*Tax*	*Book*	*Tax*
Initial Contribution	$ 10,000	$ 4,000	$ 10,000	$ 10,000
Depreciation	(500)	(0)	(500)	(400)
Sales Income	350	350	350	350
	$ 9,850	$ 4,350	$ 9,850	$ 9,950

Example 2 Reasonable Curative Allocation.

- Because the ceiling rule would cause a disparity of $ 100 between F's book and tax capital accounts, EF may properly allocate to E under paragraph (c) of this section an additional $ 100 of income from the sale of inventory for tax purposes. This allocation results in capital accounts at the end of EF's first year as follows.

	E		F	
Items	*Book*	*Tax*	*Book*	*Tax*
Initial Contribution	$ 10,000	$ 4,000	$ 10,000	$ 10,000
Depreciation	(500)	(0)	(500)	(400)
Sales Income	350	450	350	250
	$ 9,850	$ 4,450	$ 9,850	$ 9,850

7.5.3 Remedial Method

The remedial method allows partnership to create (i.e., "fabricate") income and deduction items. It is not dependent on the adequacy of the partnership items aiming to completely prevent any ceiling rule limitations. The remedial items have no effect on book capital accounts, and the calculation of book depreciation is different than under the traditional or curative method. The remedial method contribution is treated in a manner similar to a "deferred sale" and any ceiling rule limitation is offset through the creation of additional deductions and offsetting income. However, IRC section 704(c)does not prevent shifting of tax attributes among partners. Also, although rules are fairly straightforward if only one property is involved, application is much more complicated if there are multiple properties with different methods and multiple "layers." Further complexity arises from the interaction with other Code provisions, particularly section 743 and section 734.

Example 1 Remedial Allocation Method

Facts

- On January 1, L and M form partnership LM and agree that each will be allocated a 50% share of all partnership items.
- The partnership agreement provides that LM will make allocations under section 704(c) using the remedial allocation method under this paragraph (d) and that the straight-line method will be used to recover excess book basis.
- L contributes depreciable property with an adjusted tax basis of $ 4,000 and an FMV of $ 10,000.
- The property is depreciated using the straight-line method with a 10-year recovery period and has 4 years remaining on its recovery period.
- M contributes $ 10,000, which the partnership uses to purchase land. Except for the depreciation deductions, LM's expenses equal its income in each year of the 10 years commencing with the year the partnership is formed.

Years 1 through 4

- Under the remedial allocation method of this paragraph (d), LM has book depreciation for each of its first 4 years of $ 1,600 ($ 1,000 ($ 4,000 adjusted tax basis divided by the 4-year remaining recovery period) plus $ 600 ($ 6,000 excess of book value over tax basis, divided by the new 10-year recovery period)).
- For the purpose of simplifying the example, the partnership's book depreciation is determined without regard to any first-year depreciation conventions.
- Under the partnership agreement, L and M are each allocated 50% ($ 800) of the book depreciation. M is allocated $ 800 of tax depreciation and L is allocated the remaining $ 200 of tax depreciation ($ 1,000-$ 800). No remedial

allocations are made because the ceiling rule does not result in a book allocation of depreciation to M different from the tax allocation. The allocations result in capital accounts at the end of LM's first 4 years as follows:

	L		*M*	
Items	*Book*	*Tax*	*Book*	*Tax*
Initial Contribution	$ 10,000	$ 4,000	$ 10,000	$ 10,000
Depreciation	(3,200)	(800)	(3,200)	(800)
	$ 6,800	$ 3,200	$ 6,800	$ 6,800

Subsequent Years

- For each of years 5 through 10, LM has $ 600 of book depreciation ($ 6,000 excess of initial book value over adjusted tax basis divided by the 10-year recovery period that commented in year 1), but no tax depreciation.
- Under the partnership agreement, $ 600 of book depreciation is allocated equally to L and M. Because of the application of the ceiling rule in year 5, M would be allotted $ 300 of book depreciation, but no tax depreciation.
- Thus, at the end of LM's fifth year L's and M's book and tax capital accounts would be as follows:

Items	*L*		*M*	
End of year 4	$ 6,800	$ 3,200	$ 6,800	$ 6,800
Depreciation	(300)	-	(300)	-
	$ 6,500	$ 3,200	$ 6,500	$ 6,800

CHAPTER 8

Partnership Liabilities

Section 752 separates partnership liabilities into two categories: recourse liabilities and nonrecourse liabilities. Under a recourse liability, a partner generally bears the EROL for a partnership liability if the partner or related person has an obligation to make a payment to any person within the meaning of §1.752-2(b). Nonrecourse liabilities are those liabilities where only the creditor bears the EROL and, according to section 752, are those partnership liabilities for which no partner bears the EROL. In the case of nonrecourse partnership liabilities each partner's share of such liabilities is equal to his share of partnership profits.

8.1 GENERAL

Section 752 separates partnership liabilities into two categories: recourse liabilities and nonrecourse liabilities. Section 1.752-1(a)(1) provides that a partnership liability is a recourse liability to the extent that any partner or related person bears the EROL for that liability under §1.752-2. Section 1.752-1(a)(2) provides that a partnership liability is a nonrecourse liability to the extent that no partner or related person bears the EROL for that liability under §1.752-2.

Section 752 provides:

> "(a) Any increase in a partner's share of the liabilities of a partnership, or any increase in a partner's individual liabilities by reason of the assumption by such partner of partnership liabilities, shall be considered as a contribution of money by such partner to the partnership."
> "(b) Any decrease in a partner's share of the liabilities of a partnership, or any decrease in a partner's individual liabilities by reason of the assumption by the partnership of such individual liabilities, shall be considered as a distribution of money to the partner by the partnership."
> "(c) For purposes of this section, a liability to which property is subject shall, to the extent of the fair market value of such property, be considered as a liability of the owner of the property."

> "(d) Sale or exchange of an interest: In the case of a sale or exchange of an interest in a partnership, liabilities shall be treated in the same manner as liabilities in connection with the sale or exchange of property not associated with partnerships."

The transfer of property subject to a liability by a partner to a partnership, or by the partnership to a partner, shall, to the extent of the FMV of such property, be considered a transfer of the amount of the liability along with the property.[25]

When a partnership interest is sold or exchanged, the general rule for the treatment of the sale or exchange of property subject to liabilities will be applied.[26]

8.2 PARTNERSHIP RECOURSE LIABILITIES

A partner generally bears the EROL for a partnership liability if the partner or related person has an obligation to make a payment to any person within the meaning of §1.752-2(b). For purposes of determining the extent to which a partner or related person has an obligation to make a payment, an obligation to restore a deficit capital account upon liquidation of the partnership under the section 704(b) regulations is taken into account (deficit restoration obligation). Further, for this purpose, §1.752-2(b)(6) of the existing regulations presumes that partners and related persons who have payment obligations actually perform those obligations, irrespective of their net worth, unless the facts and circumstances indicate a plan to circumvent or avoid the obligation. This is known as the satisfaction presumption. However, the satisfaction presumption is subject to an anti-abuse rule in §1.752-2(j) pursuant to which a payment obligation of a partner or related person may be disregarded or treated as an obligation of another person if facts and circumstances indicate that a principal purpose of the arrangement is to eliminate the partner's EROL with respect to that obligation or create the appearance of the partner or related person bearing the EROL when the substance is otherwise. Under the existing rules, the satisfaction presumption is also subject to a disregarded entity net value requirement under §1.752-2(k) pursuant to which, for purposes of determining the extent to which a partner bears the EROL for a partnership liability, a payment obligation of a disregarded entity is taken into account only to the extent of the net value of the disregarded entity as of the allocation date that is allocated to the partnership liability.

The determination of the extent to which a partner or related person has an obligation to make a payment under §1.752-2(b)(1) is based on the facts and circumstances at the time of the determination. All statutory and contractual obligations relating to the partnership liability are taken into account for purposes of applying §1.752-2(b) including:

25. H.R. Rep. No. 1337, 83d Cong., 2d Sess., A236 (1954); S. Rep. No. 1622, 83d Cong., 2d Sess., 405 (1954).
26. H.R. Rep. No. 1337, at A236-A237; S. Rep. No. 1622, at 405.

- contractual obligations outside the partnership agreement such as guarantees, indemnifications, reimbursement agreements, and other obligations running directly to creditors, to other partners, or to the partnership;
- obligations to the partnership that are imposed by the partnership agreement, including the obligation to make a capital contribution and to restore a deficit capital account upon liquidation of the partnership; and
- payment obligations (whether in the form of direct remittances to another partner or a contribution to the partnership) imposed by state or local law, including the governing state or local law partnership statute.

8.2.1 Partnership Disclosure

A partnership must disclose to the IRS a bottom dollar payment obligation with respect to a partnership liability on a completed Form 8275, Disclosure Statement, or successor form, attached to the return of the partnership for the taxable year in which the bottom dollar payment obligation is undertaken or modified, that includes all of the following information:

- A caption identifying the statement as a disclosure of a bottom dollar payment obligation under section 752.
- An identification of the payment obligation with respect to which disclosure is made (including whether the obligation is a guarantee, a reimbursement, an indemnity, or an obligation to restore a deficit balance in a partner's capital account).
- The amount of the payment obligation.
- The parties to the payment obligation.
- A statement of whether the payment obligation is treated as recognized for purposes of this paragraph (b)(3).
- If the payment obligation is recognized under paragraph (b)(3)(ii)(B) of this section, the facts and circumstances that clearly establish that a partner or related person is liable for up to 90% of the partner's or related person's initial payment obligation and, but for an indemnity, a reimbursement agreement, or a similar arrangement, the partner's or related person's initial payment obligation would have been recognized under paragraph (b)(3).

For purposes of determining the extent to which a partner or related person has a payment obligation and the EROL, it is assumed that all partners and related persons who have obligations to make payments (a payment obligor) actually perform those obligations, irrespective of their actual net worth, unless the facts and circumstances indicate:

- a plan to circumvent or avoid the obligation; or
- that there is not a commercially reasonable expectation that the payment obligor will have the ability to make the required payments under the terms of the obligation if the obligation becomes due and payable.

Irrespective of the form of a contractual obligation, a partner is considered to bear the EROL with respect to a partnership liability, or a portion thereof, to the extent that:

- the partner or related person undertakes one or more contractual obligations so that the partnership may obtain or retain a loan;
- the contractual obligations of the partner or related person significantly reduce the risk to the lender that the partnership will not satisfy its obligations under the loan, or a portion thereof; and
- any contractual obligations whereby one of the principal purposes of using the contractual obligations is to attempt to permit partners (other than those who are directly or indirectly liable for the obligation) to include a portion of the loan in the basis of their partnership interests; or another partner, or a person related to another partner, enters into a payment obligation and a principal purpose of the arrangement is to cause the payment obligation.

8.2.2 Partnership Plan to Circumvent or Avoid Payment Obligation

In the case of a payment obligation, other than an obligation to restore a deficit capital account upon liquidation of a partnership, the IRS provides a non-exclusive list of factors that may indicate a plan to circumvent or avoid the payment obligation. The presence or absence of a factor is based on all of the facts and circumstances at the time the partner or related person makes the payment obligation or if the obligation is modified, at the time of the modification. For purposes of making such determinations the weight to be given to any particular factor depends on the particular case and the presence or absence of a factor is not necessarily indicative of whether a payment obligation is or is not recognized:

- The partner or related person is not subject to commercially reasonable contractual restrictions that protect the likelihood of payment, including, for example, restrictions on transfers for inadequate consideration or distributions by the partner or related person to equity owners in the partner or related person.
- The partner or related person is not required to provide (either at the time the payment obligation is made or periodically) commercially reasonable documentation regarding the partner's or related person's financial condition to the benefited part, including, for example, balance sheets and financial statements.
- The term of the payment obligation ends prior to the term of the partnership liability, or the partner or related person has a right to terminate its payment obligation, if the purpose of limiting the duration of the payment obligation is to terminate such payment obligation prior to the occurrence of an event or events that increase the risk of economic loss to the guarantor or benefited party (e.g., termination prior to the due date of a balloon payment or a right to terminate that can be exercised because the value of loan collateral decreases).

- There exists a plan or arrangement in which the primary obligor or any other obligor (or a person related to the obligor) with respect to the partnership liability directly or indirectly holds money or other liquid assets in an amount that exceeds the reasonably foreseeable needs of such obligor (but not taking into account standard commercial insurance, for example, casualty insurance).
- The payment obligation does not permit the creditor to promptly pursue payment following a payment default on the partnership liability, or other arrangements with respect to the partnership liability or payment obligation otherwise indicate a plan to delay collection.
- In the case of a guarantee or similar arrangement, the terms of the partnership liability would be substantially the same had the partner or related person not agreed to provide the guarantee.
- The creditor or other party benefiting from the obligation did not receive executed documents with respect to the payment obligation from the partner or related person before, or within a commercially reasonable period of time after, the creation of the obligation.

Example

- In 2020, A, B, and C form a domestic LLC that is classified as a partnership for federal tax purposes.
- Also in 2020, LLC receives a loan from a bank. A, B, and C do not bear the EROL with respect to that partnership liability, and, as a result, the liability is treated as nonrecourse under §1.752-1(a)(2) in 2020.
- In 2022, A guarantees the entire amount of the liability.
- The bank did not request the guarantee and the terms of the loan did not change as a result of the guarantee.
- A did not provide any executed documents with respect to A's guarantee to the bank. The bank also did not require any restrictions on asset transfers by A and no such restrictions exist.

Solution

In this case, the following factors indicate a plan to circumvent or avoid A's payment obligation:

(1) the partner is not subject to commercially reasonable contractual restrictions that protect the likelihood of payment, such as restrictions on transfers for inadequate consideration or equity distributions;
(2) the partner is not required to provide (either at the time the payment obligation is made or periodically) commercially reasonable documentation regarding the partner's or related person's financial condition to the benefited party;

(3) in the case of a guarantee or similar arrangement, the terms of the liability are the same as they would have been without the guarantee; and
(4) the creditor did not receive executed documents with respect to the payment obligation from the partner or related person at the time the obligation was created.

Absent the existence of other facts or circumstances that would weigh in favor of respecting A's guarantee, evidence of a plan to circumvent or avoid the obligation exists and, pursuant to paragraph (j)(3)(i) of this section, A's guarantee is not recognized under paragraph(b) of this section. As a result, LLC's liability continues to be treated as nonrecourse.

8.3 PARTNERSHIP NONRECOURSE LIABILITIES

Nonrecourse liabilities are those liabilities where only the creditor bears the EROL and, according to section 752, are those partnership liabilities for which no partner bears the EROL. In the case of nonrecourse partnership liabilities each partner's share of such liabilities is equal to his share of partnership profits.[27]

8.3.1 Bottom Dollar Payment Obligations

The final regulations provide that bottom dollar payment obligations are not recognized as recourse liabilities. A bottom dollar payment obligation is defined as being similar to one of the following three types of arrangements:

(1) With regard to guarantees, any payment obligation other than one in which the partner is or would be liable up to the full amount of such partner's payment obligation if, and to the extent that, any amount of the partnership liability is not otherwise satisfied.
(2) With regard to an indemnity, any payment obligation other than one in which the partner is or would be liable up to the full amount of such partner's payment obligation, and to the extent that any amount of the benefited party's payment obligation is recognized.
(3) An arrangement in which liabilities are incurred pursuant to a common plan, as part of a single transaction or arrangement, or as part of a series of related transactions or arrangements, and with a principal purpose of avoiding at least one of such liabilities or payment obligations with respect to such liabilities being treated as bottom dollar payment obligations.

Partnerships are required to disclose all bottom dollar payment obligations by filing Form 8275 with Form 1065 for any tax year in which a bottom dollar payment

27. Section 1.752-1(e), Income Tax Regs., T.D. 6175, 1956-1 C.B. 298, 300.

obligation is undertaken or modified. A payment obligation will not be considered a bottom dollar payment obligation solely because a maximum amount is placed on the obligation, the obligation is stated as a fixed percentage of every dollar of the partnership liability, or there is a right of proportionate contribution running between partners who are co-obligors with respect to the obligation for which each of them is jointly and severally liable. The final regulations also provide an exception to the nonrecourse liability treatment of bottom dollar payment obligations. Specifically, a bottom dollar payment obligation will be recognized as a recourse liability if the partner is liable for at least 90% of the initial payment obligation.

8.3.2 Deficit Restoration Obligations

A bottom dollar payment obligation includes, with respect to a capital contribution or deficit restoration obligation, any payment obligation other than one in which the partner would be required to make the full amount of the partner's capital contribution or to restore the full amount of the partner's deficit capital account.

8.4 COURT CASES

8.4.1 Crane v. Commissioner

In Crane v. Commissioner, 331 U.S. 1 (1947), the Court ruled that a taxpayer, who sold property encumbered by a nonrecourse mortgage (the amount of the mortgage being less than the property's value), must include the unpaid balance of the mortgage in the computation of the amount the taxpayer realized on the sale.

The facts of the case can be summarized as follows:

- Beulah B. Crane was the sole beneficiary under the will of her deceased husband. At his death in January 1932, he owned an apartment building that was then mortgaged for an amount which proved to be equal to its FMV, as determined for federal estate tax purposes.
- The widow, of course, was not personally liable on the mortgage. She operated the building for nearly seven years, hoping to turn it into a profitable venture; during that period, she claimed income tax deductions for depreciation, property taxes, interest, and operating expenses but did not make payments upon the mortgage principal.
- In computing her basis for the depreciation deductions, she included the full amount of the mortgage debt. In November 1938, with her hopes unfulfilled and the mortgage threatening foreclosure, Mrs. Crane sold the building.
- The purchaser took the property subject to the mortgage and paid Crane $ 3,000; of that amount, $ 500 went for the expenses of the sale.
- Crane reported a gain of $ 2,500 on the transaction. She reasoned that her basis in the property was zero (despite her earlier depreciation deductions based on

including the amount of the mortgage) and that the amount she realized from the sale was simply the cash she received.

- The Commissioner, on the other hand, determined that Crane realized a net taxable gain of $ 23,767.03. His theory was that the "property" acquired and sold was not the equity, as Crane claimed, but rather the physical property itself, or the owner's rights to possess, use, and dispose of it, undiminished by the mortgage.
- The T.C. agreed with the Commissioner that the building was not a capital asset.
- The T.C. upheld the Commissioner's interpretation of section 113 (a)(5) of the 1938 Act, and observed that to regard merely the taxpayer's equity in the property as her basis would lead to depreciation deductions less than the actual physical deterioration of the property, and would require the basis to be recomputed with each payment on the mortgage.
- The Court rejected Crane's claim that any loss due to depreciation belonged to the mortgagee. The effect of the Court's ruling was that the taxpayer's basis was the value of the property undiminished by the mortgage.
- Crane insisted that the nonrecourse nature of the mortgage required different treatment.
- The Court, for two reasons, disagreed. First, excluding the nonrecourse debt from the amount realized would result in the same absurdity and frustration of the Code. Second, the Court concluded that Crane obtained an economic benefit from the purchaser's assumption of the mortgage identical to the benefit conferred by the cancellation of personal debt. Because the value of the property in that case exceeded the amount of the mortgage, it was in Crane's economic interest to treat the mortgage as a personal obligation; only by so doing could she realize upon sale the appreciation in her equity represented by the $ 2,500 boot. The purchaser's assumption of the liability thus resulted in a taxable economic benefit to her, just as if she had been given, in addition to the boot, a sum of cash sufficient to satisfy the mortgage.
- On the Commissioner's appeal, the Circuit Court of Appeals reversed.
- In his opinion for the Court of Appeals, Judge Learned Hand observed:

> [The mortgagor] has all the income from the property; he manages it; he may sell it; any increase in its value goes to him; any decrease falls on him, until the value goes below the amount of the lien. ... When therefore upon a sale the mortgagor makes an allowance to the vendee of the amount of the lien, he secures a release from a charge upon his property quite as though the vendee had paid him the full price on condition that before he took title the lien should be cleared.

- The U.S. Supreme Court held that a mortgagor, not personally liable on the debt, who sold the property subject to the mortgage and for additional consideration, realizes a benefit in the amount of the mortgage as well as the boot and that the Commissioner was right in determining that petitioner realized $ 257,500.00 on the sale of this property.

8.4.2 Commissioner v. Tufts (1983)

In Commissioner v. Tuft, the question was whether the same rule applies when the unpaid amount of the nonrecourse mortgage exceeds the FMV of the property sold. The Court disinclined to overrule Crane and concluded that the same rule applies when the unpaid amount of the nonrecourse mortgage exceeds the value of the property transferred; therefore the amount of the nonrecourse liability is to be included in calculating both the basis and the amount realized on disposition. The amount of the loan, which exceeds the FMV of the property becomes irrelevant.

The key facts were as follows:

- On August 1, 1970, Clark Pelt, a builder, and his wholly owned corporation ("Clark Inc.") formed a general partnership. The purpose of the partnership was to construct a 120-unit apartment complex in Duncanville, Tex., a Dallas suburb.
- Neither Pelt nor Clark, Inc. made any capital contribution to the partnership.
- Six days later, the partnership entered into a mortgage loan agreement with the Farm & Home Savings Association (F & H). Under the agreement, F & H was committed for a $ 1,851,500 loan for the complex.
- In return, the partnership executed a note and a deed of trust in favor of F & H.
- The partnership obtained the loan on a nonrecourse basis: neither the partnership nor its partners assumed any personal liability for repayment of the loan. Pelt later admitted four friends and relatives: Tufts, Steger, Stephens, and Austin, as general partners. None of them contributed capital upon entering the partnership.
- The construction of the complex was completed in August 1971. During 1971, each partner made small capital contributions to the partnership; in 1972, however, only Pelt made a contribution. The total of the partners' capital contributions was $ 44,212.
- In each tax year, all partners claimed as income tax deductions their allocable shares of ordinary losses and depreciation. The deductions taken by the partners in 1971 and 1972 totaled $ 439,972.
- Due to these contributions and deductions, the partnership's adjusted basis in the property in August 1972 was $ 1,455,740.
- On August 28, 1972, each partner sold his partnership interest to an unrelated third party, Fred Bayles. As consideration, Bayles agreed to reimburse each partner's sale expenses up to $ 250; he also assumed the nonrecourse mortgage.
- On the date of transfer, the FMV of the property did not exceed $ 1,400,000. Each partner reported the sale on his federal income tax return and indicated that a partnership loss of $ 55,740 had been sustained.
- The Commissioner of Internal Revenue, on audit, determined that the sale resulted in a partnership capital gain of approximately $ 400,000. His theory was that the partnership had realized the full amount of the nonrecourse obligation.

- The United States T.C., in an unreviewed decision, upheld the asserted deficiencies.
- The United States Court of Appeals for the Fifth Circuit questioned the theoretical underpinnings of the Crane and reversed.
- The Supreme Court held that:

> When a taxpayer sells or disposes of property encumbered by a non-recourse obligation, the Commissioner properly requires him to include among the assets realized the outstanding amount of the obligation. The fair market value of the property is irrelevant to this calculation.

CHAPTER 9
Partnership Distribution

A distribution is a transfer of cash or property by a partnership to a partner with respect to the partner's interest in partnership capital or income. Distributions do not include loans to partners or amounts paid to partners for services or the use of property, such as rent, or guaranteed payments. If a partnership acquires a partner's debt and extinguishes the debt by distributing it to the partner, the partner recognizes capital gain or loss to the extent the FMV of the debt differs from the basis of the debt. The partner is treated as having satisfied the debt for its FMV. The basis of property received in complete liquidation of a partner's interest is the adjusted basis of the PIP reduced by any money distributed to the partner in the same transaction.

9.1 GENERAL

A distribution is a transfer of cash or property by a partnership to a partner with respect to the partner's interest in partnership capital or income. Distributions do not include loans to partners or amounts paid to partners for services or the use of property, such as rent, or guaranteed payments. Partnership distributions include the following:

- A withdrawal by a partner in anticipation of the current year's earnings.
- Distribution of the current year's or prior years' earnings not needed for working capital.
- A complete or partial liquidation of a partner's interest.
- A distribution to all partners in a complete liquidation of the partnership.

A partnership distribution is not taken into account in determining the partner's distributive share of partnership income or loss. If any gain or loss from the distribution is recognized by the partner, it must be reported on his or her return for the tax year in which the distribution is received. Money or property withdrawn by a partner in anticipation of the current year's earnings is treated as a distribution received on the last day of the partnership's tax year. A partnership generally does not recognize any gain or loss because of distributions it makes to partners. The partnership may be able to elect to adjust the basis of its undistributed property. However, a partner's adjusted basis in his or her partnership interest is decreased (but not below zero) by the money and adjusted basis of property distributed to the partner.

9.2 DISTRIBUTIONS TREATED AS A SALE OR EXCHANGE

When a partnership distributes the following items, the distribution may be treated as a sale or exchange of property rather than a distribution:

- Unrealized receivables or substantially appreciated inventory items distributed in exchange for any part of the partner's interest in other partnership property, including money.
- Other property (including money) distributed in exchange for any part of a partner's interest in unrealized receivables or substantially appreciated inventory items.[28] Inventory items of the partnership are considered to have appreciated substantially in value if, at the time of the distribution, their total FMV is more than 120% of the partnership's adjusted basis for the property. However, if a principal purpose for acquiring inventory property is to avoid ordinary income treatment by reducing the appreciation to less than 120%, that property is excluded.

9.3 PARTNER'S GAIN OR LOSS

A partner generally recognizes gain on a partnership distribution only to the extent any money (and marketable securities treated as money) included in the distribution exceeds the adjusted basis of the PIP. Any gain recognized is generally treated as capital gain from the sale of the partnership interest on the date of the distribution. If partnership property (other than marketable securities treated as money) is distributed to a partner, he or she generally does not recognize any gain until the sale or other disposition of the property.

Example

- The adjusted basis of Jo's partnership interest is $ 14,000.
- She receives a distribution of $ 8,000 cash and land that has an adjusted basis of $ 2,000 and an FMV of $ 3,000.
- Because the cash received does not exceed the basis of her partnership interest, Jo does not recognize any gain on the distribution.

28. Substantially appreciated inventory items.

- Any gain on the land will be recognized when she sells or otherwise disposes of it. The distribution decreases the adjusted basis of Jo's partnership interest to $ 4,000 ($ 14,000-($ 8,000 + $ 2,000)).

Quid? Marketable Securities Treated as Money

Generally, a marketable security distributed to a partner is treated as money in determining whether gain is recognized on the distribution. This treatment, however, does not generally apply if that partner contributed the security to the partnership or an investment partnership made the distribution to an eligible partner. The amount treated as money is the security's FMV when distributed, reduced (but not below zero) by the excess (if any) of:

(1) the partner's distributive share of the gain that would be recognized had the partnership sold all its marketable securities at their FMV immediately before the transaction resulting in the distribution, over;
(2) the partner's distributive share of the gain that would be recognized had the partnership sold all such securities it still held after the distribution at the FMV in (1).

9.4 LOSS ON DISTRIBUTION

A partner does not recognize loss on a partnership distribution unless all the following requirements are met:

- The adjusted basis of the PIP exceeds the distribution.
- The partner's entire interest in the partnership is liquidated.
- The distribution is in money, unrealized receivables, or inventory items.

9.5 DISTRIBUTION OF PARTNER'S DEBT

If a partnership acquires a partner's debt and extinguishes the debt by distributing it to the partner, the partner recognizes capital gain or loss to the extent the FMV of the debt differs from the basis of the debt. The partner is treated as having satisfied the debt for its FMV. If the issue price (adjusted for any premium or discount) of the debt exceeds its FMV when distributed, the partner may have to include the excess amount in income as canceled debt. Similarly, a deduction may be available to a corporate partner if the FMV of the debt at the time of distribution exceeds its adjusted issue price.

9.6 NET PRE-CONTRIBUTION GAIN

A partner generally must recognize gain on the distribution of property (other than money) if the partner contributed appreciated property to the partnership during the seven-year period before the distribution. The gain recognized is the lesser of the following amounts:

(1) The excess of:

(i) the FMV of the property received in the distribution, over (ii) the adjusted basis of the PIP immediately before the distribution, reduced (but not below zero) by any money received in the distribution.

The "net pre-contribution gain" of the partner: This is the net gain the partner would recognize if all the property contributed by the partner within seven years of the distribution, and held by the partnership immediately before the distribution, were distributed to another partner, other than a partner who owns more than 50% of the partnership.

The character of the gain is determined by reference to the character of the net pre-contribution gain. This gain is in addition to any gain the partner must recognize if the money distributed is more than his or her basis in the partnership.

The adjusted basis of the PIP is increased by any net pre-contribution gain recognized by the partner. Other than for purposes of determining the gain, the increase is treated as occurring immediately before the distribution.

The partnership must adjust its basis in any property the partner contributed within seven years of the distribution to reflect any gain that the partner recognizes under this rule.

However, any part of a distribution that is property the partner previously contributed to the partnership is not taken into account in determining the amount of the excess distribution or the partner's net pre-contribution gain. For this purpose, the partner's previously contributed property does not include a contributed interest in an entity to the extent its value is due to property contributed to the entity after the interest was contributed to the partnership.

9.7 PARTNER'S BASIS FOR DISTRIBUTED PROPERTY

Unless there is a complete liquidation of a partner's interest, the basis of property (other than money) distributed to the partner by a partnership is its adjusted basis to the partnership immediately before the distribution. However, the basis of the property to the partner cannot be more than the adjusted basis of his or her interest in the partnership reduced by any money received in the same transaction.

Example 1

- The adjusted basis of Emily's partnership interest is $ 30,000.
- She receives a distribution of property that has an adjusted basis of $ 20,000 to the partnership and $ 4,000 in cash.
- Her basis for the property is $ 20,000.

Example 2

- The adjusted basis of Steve's partnership interest is $ 10,000.
- He receives a distribution of $ 4,000 cash and property that has an adjusted basis to the partnership of $ 8,000.
- His basis for the distributed property is limited to $ 6,000 ($ 10,000-$ 4,000, the cash he receives).

9.8 COMPLETE LIQUIDATION OF PARTNER'S INTEREST

The basis of property received in complete liquidation of a partner's interest is the adjusted basis of the PIP reduced by any money distributed to the partner in the same transaction.

9.8.1 Partner's Holding Period

A partner's holding period for property distributed to the partner includes the period the property was held by the partnership. If the property was contributed to the partnership by a partner, then the period it was held by that partner is also included.

9.8.2 Divided Basis among Properties

If the basis of property received is the adjusted basis of the PIP (reduced by money received in the same transaction), it must be divided among the properties distributed to the partner. For property distributed after August 5, 1997, the basis is allocated using the following rules:

(1) Allocate the basis first to unrealized receivables and inventory items included in the distribution by assigning a basis to each item equal to the partnership's adjusted basis in the item immediately before the distribution. If the total of these assigned bases exceed the allocable basis, decrease the assigned bases by the amount of the excess.

(2) Allocate any remaining basis to properties other than unrealized receivables and inventory items by assigning a basis to each property equal to the partnership's adjusted basis in the property immediately before the distribution. If the allocable basis exceeds the total of these assigned bases, increase the assigned bases by the amount of the excess. If the total of these assigned bases exceeds the allocable basis, decrease the assigned bases by the amount of the excess.

9.8.3 Allocating a Basis Increase

Allocate any basis increase required in rule (2) above first to properties with unrealized appreciation to the extent of the unrealized appreciation. If the basis increase is less than the total unrealized appreciation, allocate it among those properties in proportion to their respective amounts of unrealized appreciation. Allocate any remaining basis increase among all the properties in proportion to their respective FMVs.

Example

- Eun's basis in her partnership interest is $ 55,000.
- In a distribution in liquidation of her entire interest, she receives properties A and B, neither of which is inventory or unrealized receivables.
- Property A has an adjusted basis to the partnership of $ 5,000 and an FMV of $ 40,000.
- Property B has an adjusted basis to the partnership of $ 10,000 and an FMV of $ 10,000.
- To figure her basis in each property, Eun first assigns bases of $ 5,000 to property A and $ 10,000 to property B (their adjusted bases to the partnership).
- This leaves a $ 40,000 basis increase (the $ 55,000 allocable basis minus the $ 15,000 total of the assigned bases).
- She first allocates $ 35,000 to property A (its unrealized appreciation).
- The remaining $ 5,000 is allocated between the properties based on their FMVs. $ 4,000 ($ 40,000/$ 50,000) is allocated to property A and $ 1,000 ($ 10,000/$ 50,000) is allocated to property B.
- Eun's basis in property A is $ 44,000 ($ 5,000 + $ 35,000 + $ 4,000) and her basis in property B is $ 11,000 ($ 10,000 + $ 1,000).

9.8.4 Allocating a Basis Decrease

Use the following rules to allocate any basis decrease required in rule (1) or rule (2), earlier:

(1) Allocate the basis decrease first to items with unrealized depreciation to the extent of the unrealized depreciation. If the basis decrease is less than the total unrealized depreciation, allocate it among those items in proportion to their respective amounts of unrealized depreciation.
(2) Allocate any remaining basis decrease among all the items in proportion to their respective assigned basis amounts (as decreased in (1)).

Example

- Armando's basis in his partnership interest is $ 20,000.
- In a distribution in liquidation of his entire interest, he receives properties C and D, neither of which is inventory or unrealized receivables.
- Property C has an adjusted basis to the partnership of $ 15,000 and an FMV of $ 15,000.
- Property D has an adjusted basis to the partnership of $ 15,000 and an FMV of $ 5,000.
- To figure his basis in each property, Armando first assigns bases of $ 15,000 to property C and $ 15,000 to property D (their adjusted bases to the partnership).
- This leaves a $ 10,000 basis decrease (the $ 30,000 total of the assigned bases minus the $ 20,000 allocable basis).
- He allocates the entire $ 10,000 to property D (its unrealized depreciation). Armando's basis in property C is $ 15,000 and his basis in property D is $ 5,000 ($ 15,000-$ 10,000).

9.8.5 Distributions Before August 6, 1997

For property distributed before August 6, 1997, the basis is allocated using the following rules:

(1) Allocate the basis first to unrealized receivables and inventory items included in the distribution to the extent of the partnership's adjusted basis in those items. If the partnership's adjusted basis in those items exceeded the allocable basis, allocate the basis among the items in proportion to their adjusted bases to the partnership.
(2) Allocate any remaining basis to other distributed properties in proportion to their adjusted bases to the partnership.

9.8.6 Partner's Interest More Than Partnership Basis

If the basis of a partner's interest to be divided in a complete liquidation of the partner's interest is more than the partnership's adjusted basis for the unrealized receivables and inventory items distributed, and if no other property is distributed to which the partner can apply the remaining basis, the partner has a capital loss to the extent of the remaining basis of the partnership interest.

9.8.7 Special Adjustment to Basis

A partner who acquired any part of his or her partnership interest in a sale or exchange or upon the death of another partner may be able to choose a special basis adjustment for property distributed by the partnership. To choose the special adjustment, the partner must have received the distribution within two years after acquiring the partnership interest. Also, the partnership must not have chosen the optional adjustment to basis when the partner acquired the partnership interest. If a partner chooses this special basis adjustment, the partner's basis for the property distributed is the same as it would have been if the partnership had chosen the optional adjustment to basis. However, this assigned basis is not reduced by any depletion or depreciation that would have been allowed or allowable if the partnership had previously chosen the optional adjustment. The choice must be made with the partner's tax return for the year of the distribution if the distribution includes any property subject to depreciation, depletion, or amortization. If the choice does not have to be made for the distribution year, it must be made with the return for the first year in which the basis of the distributed property is pertinent in determining the partner's income tax. A partner choosing this special basis adjustment must attach a statement to his or her tax return that the partner chooses under section 732(d) of the IRC to adjust the basis of property received in a distribution. The statement must show the computation of the special basis adjustment for the property distributed and list the properties to which the adjustment has been allocated.

Example

- Chin Ho purchased a 25% interest in X partnership for $ 17,000 cash.
- At the time of the purchase, the partnership owned inventory having a basis to the partnership of $ 14,000 and an FMV of $ 16,000.
- Thus, $ 4,000 of the $ 17,000 he paid was attributable to his share of inventory with a basis to the partnership of $ 3,500.
- Within two years after acquiring his interest, Chin Ho withdrew from the partnership and for his entire interest received cash of $ 1,500, inventory with a basis to the partnership of $ 3,500, and other property with a basis of $ 6,000.
- The value of the inventory received was 25% of the value of all partnership inventory. (It is immaterial whether the inventory he received was on hand when he acquired his interest.)

- Since the partnership from which Chin Ho withdrew did not make the optional adjustment to basis, he chose to adjust the basis of the inventory received.
- His share of the partnership's basis for the inventory is increased by $ 500 (25% of the $ 2,000 difference between the $ 16,000 FMV of the inventory and its $ 14,000 basis to the partnership at the time he acquired his interest).
- The adjustment applies only for purposes of determining his new basis in the inventory and not for purposes of partnership gain or loss on disposition.
- The total to be allocated among the properties Chin Ho received in the distribution is $ 15,500 ($ 17,000 basis of his interest- $ 1,500 cash received). His basis in the inventory items is $ 4,000 ($ 3,500 partnership basis + $ 500 special adjustment).
- The remaining $ 11,500 is allocated to his new basis for the other property he received.

9.8.8 Mandatory Adjustment

A partner does not always have a choice of making this special adjustment to basis. The special adjustment to basis must be made for a distribution of property (whether or not within two years after the partnership interest was acquired) if all the following conditions existed when the partner received the partnership interest:

- The FMV of all partnership property (other than money) was more than 110% of its adjusted basis to the partnership.
- If there had been a liquidation of the partner's interest immediately after it was acquired, an allocation of the basis of that interest under the general rules would have decreased the basis of property that could not be depreciated, depleted, or amortized and increased the basis of property that could be.
- The optional basis adjustment, if it had been chosen by the partnership, would have changed the partner's basis for the property actually distributed.

Generally, if a partner chooses a special basis adjustment and notifies the partnership, or if the partnership makes a distribution for which the special basis adjustment is mandatory, the partnership must provide a statement to the partner. The statement must provide information necessary for the partner to figure the special basis adjustment.

CHAPTER 10

Partnership Financial Statements

A partnership business must prepare and keep its financial statements: (i) the income statement, (ii) the balance sheet, (iii) the statement of changes in partners' equity and the statement of cash flows. The key difference between accounting for partnerships and accounting for general organization firms is that the earnings have to be allocated to each partner by the end of the partnership taxable year. The capital account statement is the one financial statement totally unique to partnerships. The partnership records and tracks all contributions from and distributions to each partner in the capital account. Under certain conditions, the IRS allows a capital account to be negative at the end of each fiscal year. This can occur when the cumulative distributed cash and allocated losses exceed a partner's capital contributions plus allocated income to date.

10.1 GENERAL

The financial statements of a partnership business are similar to those of a proprietorship. They are made of: (i) the income statement, (ii) the balance sheet, (iii) the statement of changes in partners' equity and the statement of cash flows. The key difference between accounting for partnerships and accounting for general organization firms is that the earnings have to be allocated to each partner, by the end of the partnership taxable year. The partnership's net profit is allocated according to the ratio of capital invested or an agreed upon fractional basis. The fractional partnerships clearly set out the percentage of earnings each partner can take home. When using the ratio of capital invested method, the partners receive a salary proportional to their percentage of equity in the firm.

10.2 CORE FINANCIAL STATEMENTS

10.2.1 Income Statement

A general partnership prepares its income statement to reflect the revenues it generated, the expenses it incurred and the resulting partnership profits. For tax purposes, partnerships often prepare an income statement that allocates income and expenses according to directions contained in a written partnership agreement or based on the contribution levels of each partner tracked in a separate capital account.

10.2.2 Balance Sheet

The balance sheet of a business that operates as a partnership has the same basic structure as the balance sheet of a corporation. Both types have three sections: assets, liabilities and equity. A partnership's balance sheet reflects assets, liabilities and partner equity. Assets include bank accounts, accounts receivable and any property owned. Liabilities include customer retainers or deposits, accounts payable, partner loans, bank lines of credit and mortgages on property. Partner, or owner, equity reflects the total contributions and withdrawals of all the partners. A partnership has to complete a Schedule L (Balance Sheet); Schedule M-1 (Reconciliation of Income) and Schedule M-2 (Analysis of Partner's Capital Accounts) unless it can satisfy cumulatively the following four requirements:

(i) The partnership's total receipts were less than $ 250,000 for the tax year.
(ii) The partnership's total assets were less than $ 1 million at the end of the tax year.
(iii) Schedule K-1 is filed with the return and furnished to the partners on or before the due date (including extensions).
(iv) The partnership is not filing or required to file Schedule M-3.

10.2.3 The Statement of Cash Flows

The cash flow statement shows the cash inflows and outflows for the partnership from operations, investing and financing. The financing section reflects changes in the partnership debt levels and in partner equity.

10.2.4 The Capital Account

The IRS requires each partnership to keep a record of: (i) the capital contributions made by a partner, (ii) the cash distributions received by a partner, and (iii) the allocations of income and loss received by a partner. The ongoing balance of this record is referred to as a "capital account." The capital account of a partnership is significant for more than one reason, but most importantly, the service relies on the capital account to ensure that distributions and allocations between or among partners were not motivated entirely by the tax advantage but rather by the economics of the underlying partnership activities.

Under certain conditions, the IRS allows a capital account to be negative at the end of each FY. This can occur when the cumulative distributed cash and allocated losses exceed a partner's capital contributions plus allocated income to date. Moreover, a negative capital account implies a disinvested position on the underlying assets of the partnership; therefore, the IRS requires assurance that the partner with a negative capital account provides restitution to cover its deficit position in the event of liquidation. In addition to the capital account, partners are also required to maintain a balance called "outside basis."

The capital account statement is the one financial statement totally unique to partnerships. The partnership records and tracks all contributions from and distributions to each partner in the capital account. The statement of partners' equity reflects the equity of each partner and summarizes the allocation of net income for the year. Most general partnerships establish and maintain separate capital account statements for each partner to prevent tracking errors. Unless otherwise stated in the partnership agreement, partnerships allocate according to the percentage ownership the capital accounts represent. Some partnerships draft statements of partners' capital to show the changes in each partner's capital account for the year or period being reported on. It has the same format as the statement of owner's equity except that it includes a column for each partner and a total column for the company rather than just one column. The statement starts with the beginning capital balance, followed by the amounts of investments made, share of net income or loss, and withdrawals made during the reporting period to determine the capital balance at the end of the period.

The balance in each partner's capital account measures that partner's interest in the book value of the business' net assets. This figure arises from contributions, earnings, drawings, and other capital transactions.

The partner's capital account analysis can be reported using tax basis, GAAP, section 704(b) book, or other methods consistent with Form 1065. Tax basis capital refers to:

(i) the amount of cash plus the tax basis of property contributed to a partnership by a partner minus the amount of cash plus the tax basis of property distributed to a partner by the partnership net income of any liabilities assumed or taken subject to in connection with such contribution or distribution, plus;

(ii) the partner's cumulative share of taxable partnership income and tax-exempt income, minus;

(iii) the partner's cumulative share of taxable loss and nondeductible, non-capital expenditures.

Example

Two partners establish a partnership. Peter contributes $ 40,000, Mark $ 60,000. As a result, Peter will receive 40% of the income or losses, Mark 60%. The firm generates $ 100,000 of profit the next year. Peter's capital account increases by $ 40,000, which is his share of the profits; Mark's increases by $ 60,000. Because neither was paid a salary but needs to pay taxes on this amount, both withdraw the full amount of their profits. The following year the firm needs additional funds for expansion. Peter contributes $ 20,000. Now his capital account reflects $ 60,000, the same as Mark's. They will now both receive 50% of the income or losses.

10.2.4.1 Capital Accounting Rules

Contribution

Generally, no gain (loss) is recognized to the partnership or any of the partners when property is contributed to the partnership in exchange for an interest in the partnership.[29] If, as a result of a transfer of property to a partnership, there is a direct or indirect transfer of money or other property to the transferring partner, the partner may have to recognize gain on the exchange. The basis to the partnership of property contributed by a partner is the adjusted basis in the hands of the partner at the time it was contributed, plus any gain recognized (under section 721(b)) by the partner at that time. Generally, if the partnership disposes of property contributed to the partnership by a partner, income, gain, loss, and deductions from that property must be allocated among the partners to take into account the difference between the property's basis and its FMV at the time of the contribution. However, if the adjusted basis of the contributed property exceeds its FMV at the time of the contribution, the built-in loss can only be taken into account by the contributing partner. For all other partners, the basis of the property in the hands of the partnership is treated as equal to its FMV at the time of the contribution (*see* section 704(c)(1)(C)). For property contributed to the partnership, the contributing partner must recognize gain or loss on a distribution of the property to another partner within seven years of being contributed. The gain or loss is equal to the amount that the contributing partner should have recognized if the property had been sold for its FMV when distributed, because of the difference between the property's basis and its FMV at the time of contribution. However, there is an exception for contribution to partnership treated as investment company. Gain is recognized when property is contributed (in exchange for an interest in the partnership) to a partnership that would be treated as an investment company if it were incorporated.

29. This rule does not apply to any gain realized on a transfer of property to a partnership that would be treated as an investment company (within the meaning of sec. 351(e)) if the partnership were incorporated.

A partnership is generally treated as an investment company if over 80% of the value of its assets is held for investment and consists of certain readily marketable items. These items include money, stocks and other equity interests in a corporation, and interests in regulated investment companies and real estate investment trusts. Whether a partnership is treated as an investment company under this test is ordinarily determined immediately after the transfer of property. This rule applies to LPs and general partnerships, regardless of whether they are privately formed or publicly syndicated.

Earnings

A partnership's distribution of cash to a partner (representing, perhaps, already-taxed income, or capital contributions) reduces the partner's adjusted basis in his partnership interest. If a cash distribution exceeds the partner's adjusted basis in his partnership interest, the excess amount is taxable to the partner. Thus, a partner may withdraw cash from a partnership without realizing any income or gain to the extent of his adjusted basis.

Drawings

The drawing account records the amount of assets that a partner takes from the partnership during the reported period. In general, only regularly allowed distributions are recorded in the drawing account with larger, more sporadic withdrawals being recorded as direct reductions to the partner's capital balance. Partnership distributions include the following:

- A withdrawal by a partner in anticipation of the current year's earnings.
- A distribution of the current year's or prior years' earnings not needed for working capital.
- A complete or partial liquidation of a partner's interest.
- A distribution to all partners in a complete liquidation of the partnership.

A partnership distribution is not taken into account in determining the partner's distributive share of partnership income or loss. If any gain or loss from the distribution is recognized by the partner, it must be reported on his or her return for the tax year in which the distribution is received. Money or property withdrawn by a partner in anticipation of the current year's earnings is treated as a distribution received on the last day of the partnership's tax year.

Example

- After graduating from Boston University, Orion decided to create her own LLP.
- Partner Orion originally contributed $ 50,000 to the partnership.
- Partner Orion was allocated $ 35,000 of its subsequent profits and has previously received a distribution of $ 20,000.

Task: Compute the ending balance of Orion's Capital account

Answer: The ending balance of partner Orion's capital accounted is calculated as follows:

$ 50,000 initial contribution + $ 35,000 profit allocation – $ 20,000 distribution = $ 65,000 ending balance

10.3 PARTNER'S OUTSIDE BASIS

A partner outside basis is similar to an adjusted basis of a capital asset. The outside basis tracks the tax position of a partner's investment in its partnership interest. That is, if a partner were to sell its position in the partnership to another party, or if the partnership were to liquidate, the amount of the partner's outside basis would reduce its taxable gain. Should its partnership interest be worth less than its outside basis amount, then the partner would incur a taxable loss equal to the difference between the sale amount and its outside basis. The outside basis and the capital account have very similar calculations. Both include capital contributions, cash distributions, and allocations of income and loss. However, the outside basis also includes a share of any debt that the partner has adopted as part of its partnership investment. And, unlike a capital account, the outside basis can never be negative at the end of a FY. To prevent a negative basis, a partner must either suspend any allocated losses, or pay taxes on distributions received in excess of his basis. In either situation, the partner's capital account necessarily differs from its outside basis.

Another important difference between the two accounts is in the nature of a partner's contribution to the partnership. If a partner contributes property instead of cash, then the partner's adjusted basis in the property at the time of contribution is represented in its outside basis. By contrast, the FMV of the property at the time of the contribution is included in the partner's capital account. If the FMV is greater than the adjusted basis, then the contributing partner recognizes the gain in the pattern of the remaining original depreciation schedule at the time of contribution. These taxable deferred gain charges are represented in his outside basis but are not included in the partner's capital account.

Example: Partner outside basis

- Amouly and Brenda created a partnership, AB LLP.
- Amouly contributed a land with a tax basis of $ 10,000 and an FMV of $ 50,000 to the partnership.
- Brenda contributed $ 50,000 cash.

Task: Determine Amouly and Brenda's outside basis in the partnership

[Outside basis represents each partner's basis in the partnership interest. Each partner owns a share of the partnership's inside basis for all of its assets, and all partners should maintain a record of their respective outside bases].

Answer: (1) Amouly's outside basis: $ 10,000 (he tax basis if the land); and (2) Brenda's outside basis: $ 50,000

10.4 PARTNERSHIP RETAINED EARNINGS

When partners leave profits in the business instead of withdrawing them, these profits are known as retained income. The IRS requires the partners to pay taxes on this partnership income as if it had been distributed. Unless otherwise stated in the partnership agreement explaining the percentages of retained earnings allocated to each partner, in proportion to their percentage of ownership in the company, retained earnings should be listed on each partner's individual 1040 form.

CHAPTER 11
Partnership Tax Reporting

The partnership must furnish copies of Schedule K-1 (Form 1065) to the partner. Certain partnerships with more than 100 partners are required to file Form 1065, Schedules K-1, and related forms and schedules electronically. A partner must keep records of his/her Schedule K-1 and not file it with his/her tax return unless he/she is specifically required to do so. The partnership files a copy of Schedule K-1 (Form 1065) with the IRS. The K-1 form lists the partner's name, address and percentage share of profits, losses, capital and liabilities.

11.1 GENERAL

A partnership must file an annual information return to report the income, deductions, gains, losses, etc., from its operations, but it does not pay income tax. Instead, it "passes through" profits or losses to its partners. Each partner reports its share of the partnership's income or loss on its personal tax return. Partners are not employees and should not be issued a Form W-2. The partnership must furnish copies of Schedule K-1 (Form 1065) to the partner. Certain partnerships with more than 100 partners are required to file Form 1065, Schedules K-1, and related forms and schedules electronically. For tax years beginning on or after July 2, 2019, a religious or apostolic organization exempt from income tax under section 501(d) must file Form 1065 electronically. Other partnerships generally have the option to file electronically.

11.2 FORM 1065: U.S. RETURN OF PARTNERSHIP INCOME

Generally, a domestic partnership must file Form 1065 by the 15th day of the 3rd month following the date its tax year ended as shown at the top of Form 1065. For calendar year partnerships, the due date is March 15. If the due date falls on a Saturday, Sunday, or legal holiday in the District of Columbia or the state in which you file your return, a return filed by the next day that is not a Saturday, Sunday, or legal holiday will be treated as timely. Calendar year partnerships may therefore timely file their return for the 2019 partnership year by March 16, 2020. A partnership seeking extension must file Form 7004 to request an extension of time. Within Form 1065, the partnership reports its total income less the deductions thereof. It also reports deductions such as salaries, guaranteed payments to partners, rent, repairs, taxes, depreciation and employee benefit programs. Form 1065 contains several schedules: Schedule B includes a series of questions about the partnership—from the types of partners to ownership of corporate shares to types of distributions made. Schedule K is a schedule of income and expenses that forms the basis for the K-1 forms that a partnership issues to its shareholders. Schedule L is a balance sheet. Some partnerships are also required to complete Schedules M-1, M-2 and/or M-3. The return must be signed by a general partner.

11.3 SCHEDULE K-1

The partnership uses Schedule K-1 to report partner's share of the partnership's income, deductions, credits, etc. A partner must keep records of his/her Schedule K-1 and not file it with his/her tax return unless he/she is specifically required to do so. The partnership files a copy of Schedule K-1 (Form 1065) with the IRS. The K-1 form lists the partner's name, address and percentage share of profits, losses, capital and liabilities. It then lists the partner's share of ordinary business income or loss, rental income or loss and interest income. It also includes the partner's self-employment income, credits and distributions. The amount of loss and deduction a partner may claim on his/her tax return may be less than the amount reported on Schedule K-1. It is the partner's responsibility to consider and apply any applicable limitations. A partner in a partnership that has not elected out of the centralized partnership audit (CPA) regime enacted by the Bipartisan Budget Act of 2015 (BBA) must report the items shown on his Schedule K-1 (and any attached statements) the same way that the partnership treated the items on its return.

If a partner's treatment on his/her original or amended return is inconsistent with the partnership's treatment, or if the partnership was required to but has not filed a return, a partner must file Form 8082, Notice of Inconsistent Treatment or Administrative Adjustment Request (AAR), with his/her original or amended return to identify and explain any inconsistency. A partner who failed to require and file Form 8082 may be subject to the accuracy-related penalty. This penalty is in addition to any tax that results from making his/her amount or treatment of the item consistent with that shown on the partnership's return. Any deficiency that results from making the amounts consistent may be assessed immediately. Changes in a partner's tax liability with respect to affected items that require partner level determinations are computational adjustments subject to deficiency procedures. Nevertheless, any penalty, addition to tax, or additional amount that relates to an adjustment to a partnership item may be directly assessed following a partnership proceeding, based on determinations in that proceeding, regardless of whether partner level determinations are required.

11.4 PARTNERSHIP STATE TAX RETURNS

Some states require partnerships to file a state tax return. Depending on the state, partnerships may be required to pay franchise, excise or sales taxes.

A franchise tax is a government tax charged by some U.S. states to certain business organizations such as corporations and partnerships with a nexus in the state. A franchise tax is not based on income. Rather, the typical franchise tax calculation is based on the net worth of or capital held by the entity.

Excise taxes are taxes paid when purchases are made on a specific good, such as gasoline. Excise taxes are often included in the price of the product. There are also excise taxes on activities, such as on wagering or on highway usage by trucks. One of the major components of the excise program is motor fuel.

A sales tax is a tax paid to a governing body for the sales of certain goods and services. Usually laws allow the seller to collect funds for the tax from the consumer at the point of purchase. When a tax on goods or services is paid to a governing body directly by a consumer, it is usually called a use tax.

CHAPTER 12

Partnership Liquidation and Termination

For income tax purposes, a retiring partner or successor in the interest of a deceased partner is treated as a partner until his or her interest in the partnership has been completely liquidated. A partnership terminates when all its operations are discontinued and no part of any business, financial operation, or venture is continued by any of its partners in a partnership. The partnership's tax year ends on the date of termination. The date of termination is the date the partnership completes the winding up of its affairs. If a partnership is terminated before the end of what would otherwise be its tax year, Form 1065 must be filed for the short period, which is the period from the beginning of the tax year through the date of termination.

12.1 GENERAL

A partnership terminates when all its operations are discontinued and no part of any business, financial operation, or venture is continued by any of its partners in a partnership. The date of termination is the date the partnership completes the winding up of its affairs.

12.2 LIQUIDATION AT PARTNER'S RETIREMENT OR DEATH

Payments made by the partnership to a retiring partner or successor in the interest of a deceased partner in return for the partner's entire interest in the partnership may have to be allocated between payments in liquidation of the partner's interest in partnership property and other payments. The partnership's payments include an assumption of the partner's share of partnership liabilities treated as a distribution of money.

For income tax purposes, a retiring partner or successor in the interest of a deceased partner is treated as a partner until his or her interest in the partnership has been completely liquidated.

12.2.1 Liquidating Payments

Payments made in liquidation of the interest of a retiring or deceased partner in exchange for his or her interest in partnership property are considered share or guaranteed payment that could give rise to a deduction for the partnership. However, payments made for the retiring or deceased partners' share of partnership's unrealized receivables or goodwill are not treated as made in exchange for partnership property if both the following tests are met:

- Capital is not a material income-producing factor for the partnership.
- The retiring or deceased partner was a general partner in the partnership.

However, this rule does not apply to payments for goodwill to the extent that the partnership agreement provides for a reasonable payment to a retiring partner for goodwill. Unrealized receivables include, to the extent not previously includible in income under the method of accounting used by the partnership, any rights (contractual or otherwise) to payment for: (1) goods delivered, or to be delivered, to the extent the proceeds therefrom would be treated as amounts received from the sale or exchange of property other than a capital asset; or (2) services rendered or to be rendered.

12.2.2 Partners' Valuation

Generally, the partners' valuation of a partner's interest in partnership property in an arm's length agreement will be treated as correct. If the valuation reflects only the partner's net interest in the property (total assets minus liabilities), it must be adjusted so that both the value of, and the basis for, the partner's interest includes the partner's share of partnership liabilities.

12.2.3 Gain or Loss on Distribution

Upon the receipt of the distribution, the retiring partner or successor in the interest of a deceased partner will recognize gain only to the extent that any money (and marketable securities treated as money) distributed is more than the partner's adjusted basis in the partnership. The partner will recognize a loss only if the distribution is in money, unrealized receivables, and inventory items. No loss is recognized if any other property is received.

12.2.4 Other Payments

Payments made by the partnership to a retiring partner or successor in the interest of a deceased partner that are not made in exchange for an interest in partnership property are treated as distributive shares of partnership income or guaranteed payments. This rule applies regardless of the time over which the payments are to be made. It applies to payments made for the partner's share of unrealized receivables and goodwill not treated as a distribution. If the amount is based on partnership income, the payment is taxable as a distributive share of partnership income. The payment retains the same character when reported by the recipient that it would have had if reported by the partnership. If the amount is not based on partnership income, it is treated as a guaranteed payment.

The recipient reports guaranteed payments as ordinary income. These payments are included in income by the recipient for his or her tax year that includes the end of the partnership tax year for which the payments are a distributive share or in which the partnership is entitled to deduct them as guaranteed payments. Former partners who continue to make guaranteed periodic payments to satisfy the partnership's liability to a retired partner after the partnership is terminated can deduct the payments as a business expense in the year paid.

12.3 PARTNERSHIP TERMINATION

A partnership terminates when all its operations are discontinued and no part of any business, financial operation, or venture is continued by any of its partners in a partnership. The partnership's tax year ends on the date of termination. The date of termination is the date the partnership completes the winding up of its affairs. If a partnership is terminated before the end of what would otherwise be its tax year, Form 1065 must be filed for the short period, which is the period from the beginning of the tax year through the date of termination. The return is due the 15th day of the 3rd month following the date of termination.

12.4 LIQUIDATION AT PARTNER'S RETIREMENT OR DEATH

Payments made by the partnership to a retiring partner or successor in the interest of a deceased partner in return for the partner's entire interest in the partnership may have to be allocated between payments in liquidation of the partner's interest in partnership property and other payments. The partnership's payments include an assumption of the partner's share of partnership liabilities treated as a distribution of money. For income tax purposes, a retiring partner or successor in the interest of a deceased partner is treated as a partner until his or her interest in the partnership has been completely liquidated. Payments made in liquidation of the interest of a retiring or deceased partner in exchange for his or her interest in partnership property are considered a distribution, not a distributive share or guaranteed payment that could give rise to a deduction (or its equivalent) for the partnership.

12.4.1 Liquidating Payments

A partnership can make payments to a retiring or a deceased partner's successor in interest under IRC section 736. A liquidation of a partner's entire interest by means of a distribution or series of distributions. Just like with a current distribution, a partnership making a liquidating distribution does not recognize any gain or loss.

12.4.2 Unrealized Receivables and Goodwill

Payments made for the retiring or deceased partner's share of the partnership's unrealized receivables or goodwill are not treated as made in exchange for partnership property if both of the following tests are met:

- Capital is not a material income-producing factor for the partnership.
- The retiring or deceased partner was a general partner in the partnership.

Unrealized receivables include, to the extent not previously includible in income under the method of accounting used by the partnership, any rights (contractual or otherwise) to payment for: (1) goods delivered, or to be delivered, to the extent the proceeds therefrom would be treated as amounts received from the sale or exchange of property other than a capital asset; or (2) services rendered or to be rendered.

CHAPTER 13
Publicly Traded Partnership

A PTP is a business organization owned by two or more co-owners whose shares are regularly traded on an established securities market. A PTP is a type of LP managed by two or more general partners that can be individuals, corporations or other partnerships, and that is capitalized by limited partners who provide capital but have no management role in the partnership. The investor owns an interest in a partnership and is treated as a limited partner (or a member, in the case of a LLC) of a flow-through entity. A cash distribution from a PTP, although it is not currently taxable, will reduce the owner's tax basis in the partnership interest. If the partner's entire interest in the PTP is completely disposed of, any unused losses are allowed in full in the year of disposition. If the investor has an overall gain from a PTP, the net gain is nonpassive income.

13.1 GENERAL

A PTP[30] is a business organization owned by two or more co-owners whose shares are regularly traded on an established securities market. A PTP is a type of LP managed by two or more general partners that can be individuals, corporations or other partnerships, and that is capitalized by limited partners who provide capital but have no management role in the partnership. PTPs have been in existence since 1981 and were first created to add liquidity to partnership investments. Apache Corporation was the first in the United States to form a PTP in 1981. Apache's success drew other oil and gas companies to the PTP structure. A number of companies in the finance, investment and real estate industries operate as MLPs, such as Alliance Bernstein, Apollo Global Management, The Blackstone Group, Brookfield Property Partners, The Carlyle Group, Icahn Enterprises, and Och-Ziff Capital Management. A share in an MLP is called a unit, and MLP shareholders are known as unitholders. MLPs can be found on the New

30. Publicly traded partnerships are also referred to as MLPs.

York and NASDAQ exchanges, as well as many regional exchanges. They combine the affordability and liquidity of corporate stocks and bonds with the advantages of investing in a partnership. Because MLPs are not subject to corporate taxation, they act as pass-through entities. Limited partners may also record a prorated share of the MLP's depreciation on their own tax forms to reduce liability. Apache Corporation was the first in the United States to form a PTP in 1981 (Figures 13.1 and 13.2).

Figure 13.1 MLPs by Industry Group (1990-2016)

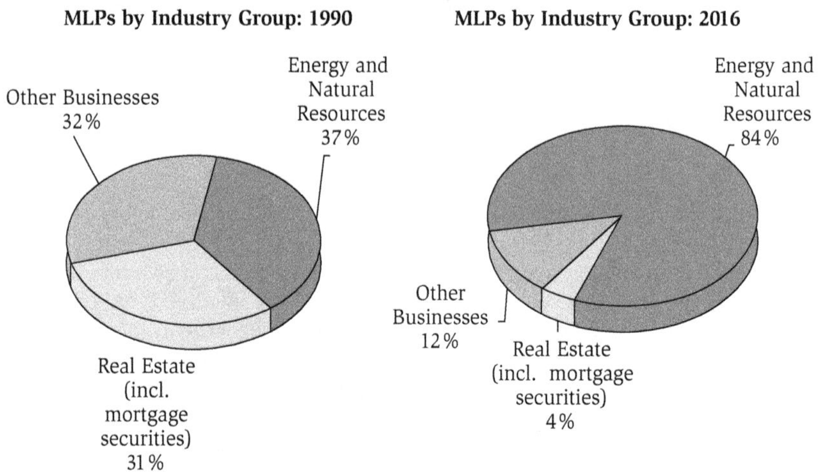

Source: © 2016 Master Limited Partnership Association.

Figure 13.2 Natural Resource MLPs: Industry Changes (1990-2016)

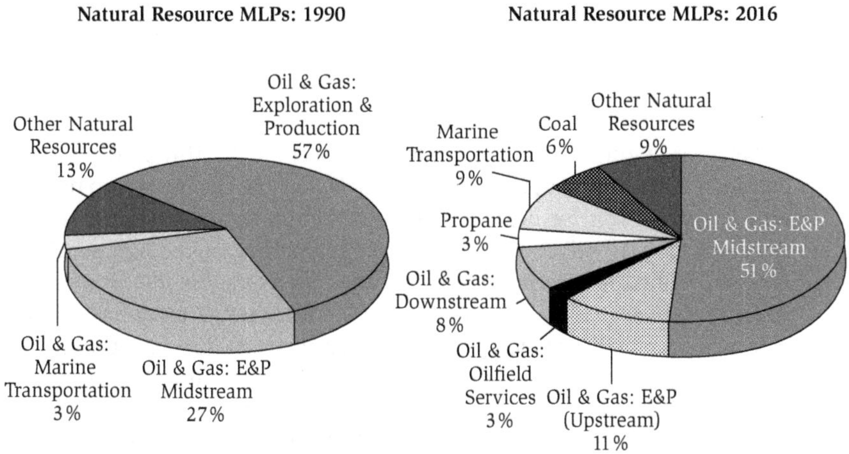

Source: © 2016 Master Limited Partnership Association.

13.2 GROSS INCOME REQUIREMENTS

Under IRS section 7704, a PTP must meet the gross income requirements for any taxable year when 90% or more of the gross income of such partnership for such taxable year consists of qualifying income. Qualifying income is generally passive-type income such as interest, dividends, and rent. However, section 7704(d)(1)(E) provides that income and gains derived from the exploration, development, mining or production, processing, refining, transportation, or the marketing of any mineral or natural resource (a "Qualifying Activity") also constitute qualifying income:

- Interest: Interest shall not be treated as qualifying income if: (a) such interest is derived in the conduct of a financial or insurance business, or (b) such interest would be excluded from the term "interest" under section 856(f).
- Dividends.
- Real property rents: Under IRC section 7704(d)(3)(A), the term "real property rent" means amounts which would qualify as rent from real property under section 856(d): (a) if such section is applied without regard to paragraph (2)(C) thereof (relating to independent contractor requirements); and (b) stock owned, directly or indirectly, by or for a partner would not be considered as owned under section 318(a)(3)(A) by the partnership unless 5% or more (by value) of the interests in such partnership are owned, directly or indirectly, by or for such partner.
- Gain from the sale or other disposition of real property: IRC section 1221 defines "capital asset" as property held by the taxpayer, whether or not it is

connected with the taxpayer's trade or business. However, property used in a taxpayer's trade or business and of a character that is subject to the allowance for depreciation provided in section 167 is not a capital asset. In the case of the sale or other disposition of real property described in section 1221(a)(1), gross income shall not be reduced by inventory costs.

- Income and gains derived from the exploration, development, mining or production, processing, refining, transportation, or the marketing of any mineral or natural resource: Under IRC section 7704(d)(1)(E), the term "mineral or natural resource" means any product of a character with respect to which a deduction for depletion is allowable under IRC section 611.[31] The definition of "gas, oil, or products thereof" includes gasoline, kerosene, No. 2 fuel oil, refined lubricating oils, diesel fuel, methane, butane, propane, and similar products that are recovered from petroleum refineries or field facilities; it is not intended to encompass oil or gas products that are produced by additional processing beyond that of petroleum refineries or field facilities, such as plastics or similar petroleum derivatives. There is no general requirement that the mineral or natural resource be from deposits in the United States. A mineral or natural resource does not include soil, sod, dirt, turf, water, or mosses, nor does it include minerals from seawater, the air, or similar inexhaustible sources. Moreover, the income must be derived from the limited functions of exploration, development, mining, production, processing, refining, transportation, or marketing of a mineral or natural resource or industrial-source carbon dioxide or for the transportation or storage of certain fuels. There is no requirement that the PTP owns the mineral or natural resource, industrial-source carbon dioxide, or certain defined fuels, only that it derives certain income or gains from it.
- Any gain from the sale or disposition of a capital asset (or property described in section 1231(b)) held for the production of income.
- Income and gains from commodities (not described in section 1221(a)(1)) or futures, forwards, and options with respect to commodities.

13.3 DISTRIBUTIONS SUBJECT TO NRA WITHHOLDING

MLPs pay their investors through quarterly required distributions, the amount of which is stated in the partnership agreement, or contract, between the limited partners (the investors) and the general partner (the managers). The distribution paid by MLPs is equivalent to the dividend paid by C corporations. In the partnership agreement, the distribution is typically defined as all available cash flow, less a reserve which is determined by the general partner. Typically, the higher the quarterly distributions paid to limited partners, the higher the management fee paid to the general partner.

31. IRS Final Regulations T.D 9817 under sec. 7704(d)(1)(E).

13.3.1 PTP as a Nominee

The PTP must withhold tax on any actual distributions of money or property to foreign partners. In the case of a partnership that receives a partnership distribution from another partnership (a tiered partnership), the distribution also includes the tax withheld from that distribution. If the distribution is in property other than money, the partnership cannot release the property until it has enough funds to pay over the withholding tax. A PTP that complies with these withholding requirements satisfies the requirements discussed under U.S. Real Property Interest. Distributions subject to withholding include:

- the FMV of U.S. real property interests distributed to a partner and potentially subject to withholding;
- amounts subject to NRA withholding, and
- amounts not subject to NRA withholding because the distributee is a partnership or is a foreign corporation that has made an election to be treated as a domestic corporation.

13.3.2 Excluded Amounts

Partnership distributions are first considered to be paid out of the following types of income in the order listed. To the extent the partnership has this type of income, it is excluded from the distributions subject to withholding:

- Amounts of non-ECI (also known as Fixed, Determinable, Annual, Periodical) distributed by the partnership and subject to NRA withholding.
- Amounts attributable to recurring dispositions of crops and timber that are subject to NRA withholding.
- Amounts attributable to the disposition of a U.S. real property interest subject to the withholding rules discussed under U.S. Real Property Interest.

13.4 TAX TREATMENT FOR INVESTORS

The investor owns an interest in a partnership and is treated as a limited partner (or a member, in the case of an LLC) of a flow-through entity. A cash distribution from a PTP, although it is not currently taxable, will reduce the owner's tax basis in the partnership interest.[32] For an individual shareholder, qualified dividends are taxed at a favorable maximum tax rate and, for a corporate shareholder, there is a dividend exclusion of at least 50% for dividends from domestic corporations.

There are three bases that must be maintained for an interest in a PTP: the tax basis, the at-risk basis, and the Alternative Minimum Tax (AMT) basis. All of these are

32. IRC sec. 733.

updated for the partner's distributive share of items that flow through annually from the partnership including, but not limited to, the partner's share of income, losses, money distributions, additional investments, and share of partnership liabilities.[33] As of 2018, individual investors and other non-corporate taxpayers are allowed to claim the new qualified business income deduction under section 199A. To that end, PTPs will be required to report the information necessary to calculate the deduction to investors on Schedule K-1.

13.4.1 The Investor Tax Basis

Investors in a PTP need to keep a record of their tax bases of the PTP investment from the time of purchase until the time of sale. That is because the investor's basis in the PTP is the starting point from which future gains and losses on the investment are calculated. First, the investor's tax basis is decreased by the amount of the cash distributions he received from the PTP. Next, the investor's basis is increased by his share of a PTP's taxable income (or decreased by his share of a PTP's taxable losses).

Example 1

- On January 1, 2018, Boguslawa made an investment in Miranda PTP by purchasing 200 units for $ 10 per unit.
- By the end of FY 2019, Boguslawa received tax documents (called a Schedule K-1) noting that she received $ 200 in cash distributions over the course of the year. The tax documents also stated that Boguslawa's pro rata share of taxable income before depreciation was $ 800, with the yearly amortization of $ 400.

Task: Compute Boguslawa tax basis

- Initial investor		$ 2,000
- Cash distributions		($ 200)
- Taxable income before depreciation	$ 800	
- Depreciation	($ 400)	
- Taxable income/loss		$ 400
- Adjusted tax basis		$ 1,800

An investor selling his interest in a PTP needs to compute his gain or loss. The taxable gain is the difference between the sales price and the adjusted tax basis. However, this entire gain is not taxed at the same rate and must be split into two components.

33. IRC secs. 705, 733, and 752.

First, the portion of the gain that is attributable to depreciation is taxed at ordinary income rates (called "recapture"). This information is provided in a supplemental sales schedule of the K-1 package (we look more closely at the K-1 in the next section). Second, the remainder of the gain (the difference between the sale price and tax basis minus the ordinary gain reflected on the K-1 sales schedule) is the capital gain and is taxed at the applicable capital gains tax rate, depending on the holding period.

Example 2

- On January 1, 2018, Boguslawa made an investment in Miranda PTP by purchasing 200 units for $ 10 per unit.
- In 2019, Boguslawa sold the 200 units at 15 per unit, for a total price of $ 3,000.

Task: Compute the capital gain or loss

Sale proceed:		$ 3,000
Tax Basis:		(1,800)
Capital Gain:		$ 1,200
Ordinary gain:	$ 400	
Capital Gain:	$ 800	

13.4.2 The Investor's At-Risk-Basis

At-risk rules are tax shelter laws that limit the amount of allowable deductions that an individual or closely held corporation can claim for tax purposes as a result of engaging in specific activities—referred to as at-risk activities—that can result in financial losses. A taxpayer's amount at risk is measured annually at the end of the tax year.[34] At-risk basis is the cumulative result of a taxpayer's: (1) contributions and distributions of cash and the adjusted basis of property contributed; (2) borrowings to the extent the taxpayer is liable for repayment or has pledged property, other than property used in the activity, as security for the borrowed amounts (recourse debts); (3) borrowings in connection with holding real property if no person is liable for repayment (qualified nonrecourse debts); and (4) the excess of pass-through items of income over deductions from the activity.[35] However, a partner shall not be considered personally liable for recourse debts if the partner is not considered the payer of last resort.[36]

34. IRC sec. 465(a)(1).
35. IRC sec. 465(b) and Prop. Regs. sec. 1.465-22.
36. *Hubert Enterprises*, T.C. Memo. 2008-46, supplementing 125 T.C. 72 (2005), aff'd in part and remanded, 230 Fed. Appx. 526 (6th Cir. 2007).

At-risk rules have been manipulated by some unscrupulous investors in the past by increasing their debts at the end of the taxable year to increase the amount of deductions available. To combat such a manipulation, the IRS has laid down factors to consider in reaching out the conclusion whether to include these debts or not. These factors include the time between the increase and decrease of debt, what normal business practices dictate, and contractual agreements between the parties.[37]

IRC section 465(e) allows investors, in certain situations, to recapture previously recognized losses. That is often the case with a change in the character of partnership debt or a reduction in the amount of debt. If a recourse debt is converted to a nonrecourse debt, the conversion will affect the at-risk basis[38] calculation for the partners, both directly by the characterization shift (nonrecourse debt does not provide at-risk basis) and indirectly by its effect on debt allocation. Recapture can also occur when the partnership makes distributions to the partners, reducing their amount at risk. It is worthy to note that if a partnership has had income in excess of deductions throughout its existence (and, thus, has never had a section 465(d) loss), there would be no recapture even if a partnership distribution reduces the at-risk basis below zero, because the taxpayer has no prior loss to recapture.[39]

Example

- In 2016, Robert Green, Carol White invested in Regal PTP.
- Regal PTP has reported income in excess of deductions for 2016, 2017, and 2018.
- By the end of 2018, Regal PTP has nonrecourse debt secured by solar energy equipment.
- At the same time, Carol White has an at-risk basis composed of a cash contribution of $ 50,000 and three years of his share of earnings totaling $ 10,000, for a total at-risk basis of $ 60,000, and a tax basis of $ 80,000 (including nonrecourse debt of $ 20,000).
- If Regal PTP distributes $ 70,000 to Carol White, the at-risk basis is reduced to $ 10,000, while his tax basis is reduced to $ 10,000.
- Carol White has no section 465(e) recapture because there have been no previously allocated losses.

13.4.3 The Investor AMT Basis

IRC section 55 imposes an AMT on all taxpayers. Congress' purpose was to tax those with substantial economic income who avoided the regular tax through exclusions,

37. IRC sec. 465(a)(1) (Prop. Regs. sec. 1.465-4(b)).
38. Prop. Regs. sec. 1.465-22.
39. IRC sec. 465(e)(2).

deductions and credits. The AMT computation begins with taxable income and then makes these adjustments provided by IRC sections 56, 57 and 58.

13.5 DISPOSITION OF PTP INTERESTS

If the partner's entire interest in the PTP is completely disposed of, any unused losses are allowed in full in the year of disposition. If the investor has an overall gain from a PTP, the net gain is nonpassive income. It is important to figure the nonpassive income because it must be included in modified adjusted gross income to figure the special allowance for active participation in a non-PTP rental real estate activity on Form 8582.

13.6 INVESTOR TAX-PLANNING STRATEGIES

There are three primary ways an investor can invest in PTPs: (i) investing in units of individual PTPs, (ii) investing in a PTP Exchange-Traded Funds (ETFs) or mutual funds, and (iii) investing in a PTP Exchange-Traded Note.

To avoid many of the tax implication pitfalls, investors may consider using a corporate investment, such as an ETF that holds interests in a number of PTPs. In this case, the investor's ownership interest would be similar to that of an investment in corporate stock; there would be no flow-through consequences; and at the time of the sale, section 751(a) would not apply, making any gain or loss recognized as a capital gain or loss. This alternative allows investors to invest in PTPs without the complex and involved tax reporting and recordkeeping requirements. The distributions from the ETF are often return-of-basis distributions that only result in a larger capital gain when the ETF is sold.[40]

13.7 PTP FINANCIAL STATEMENTS

Table 13.1 PTP Statement of Assets and Liabilities

Statement of Assets and Liabilities (unaudited) May 31, 2018	
Assets:	
Investments, at value (Cost—$ 1,409,270,747)	$ 1,652,585,024
Income tax receivable	3,376,474
Dividends and distributions receivable	529,799
Interest receivable	33,801
Prepaid expenses	66,256
Total Assets	***1,656,591,354***

40. Section 301(c)(2).

Statement of Assets and Liabilities (unaudited) May 31, 2018	
Liabilities:	
Senior secured notes (net of deferred debt issuance and offering costs of $ 1,737,363) (Note 6)	368,262,637
Deferred tax liability (Note 9)	117,068,548
Loan payable (Note 5)	73,000,000
Mandatory redeemable preferred stock ($ 100,000 liquidation value per share; 550 shares issued and outstanding) (net of deferred offering costs of $ 767,485) (Note 7)	54,232,515
Interest payable	5,862,794
Investment management fee payable	1,273,676
Distributions payable to mandatory redeemable preferred stockholders	81,497
Directors' fees payable	14,474
Accrued expenses	329,515
Total Liabilities	***620,125,656***
Total Net Assets Applicable to Common Shareholders	**$ 1,036,465,698**
Net Assets Applicable to Common Shareholders:	
Common stock par value ($ 0.001 par value, 70,414,962 shares issued and outstanding; 100,000,000 shares authorized)	$ 70,415
Paid-in capital in excess of par value	782,986,955
Accumulated net investment loss, net of income taxes	(99,455,331)
Accumulated net realized gain on investments, net of income taxes	166,562,606
Net unrealized appreciation on investments, net of income taxes	186,301,053
Total Net Assets Applicable to Common Shareholders	**$ 1,036,465,698**
Common Shares Outstanding	70,414,962
Net Asset Value Per Common Share	$ 14.72

Table 13.2 PTP Statement of Operations

Statement of Operations (Unaudited) for the Six Months Ended May 31, 2018

Statement of Operations (Unaudited) for the Six Months Ended May 31, 2018	
Investment Income:	
Dividends and distributions	$ 64,293,407
Return of capital (Note 1(e))	(55,009,223)
Net Dividends and Distributions	**9,284,184**
Interest	120,049
Less: Foreign taxes withheld	(6,962)
Total Investment Income	***9,397,271***
Expenses:	
Interest expense (Notes 5, 6 and 7)	7,765,213
Investment management fee (Note 2)	7,557,832
Distributions to mandatory redeemable preferred stockholders (Notes 1 and 7)	1,099,438
Amortization of debt issuance and offering costs (Note 6)	168,123
Directors' fees	134,793
Audit and tax fees	133,792
Legal fees	107,883
Transfer agent's fees	105,853
Amortization of preferred stock offering costs (Note 7)	80,733
Commitment fees (Note 5)	57,090
Franchise taxes	47,369
Fund accounting fees	43,560
Shareholder reports	19,135
Stock exchange listing fees	17,931
Insurance	7,731
Rating agency fees	7,447
Custody fees	6,669
Miscellaneous expenses	67,380
Total Expenses	***17,427,972***
Net Investment Loss, Before Income Taxes	**(8,030,701)**
Net current and deferred tax benefit (Note 9)	37,560,439
Net Investment Income, Net of Income Taxes	**29,529,738**
Realized and Unrealized Gain (Loss) on Investments (Notes 1, 3 and 9):	
Net Realized Gain (Loss) from:	

Statement of Operations (Unaudited) for the Six Months Ended May 31, 2018	
Investment transactions	12,560,886
Deferred tax expense (Note 9)	(3,127,642)
Net Realized Gain, Net of Income Taxes	***9,433,244***
Change in Net Unrealized Appreciation (Depreciation) from:	
Investments	61,049,056
Deferred tax benefit (Note 9)	10,502,591
Change in Net Unrealized Appreciation (Depreciation), Net of Income Taxes	***71,551,647***
Net Gain on Investments, Net of Income Taxes	**80,984,891**
Increase in Net Assets Applicable to Common Shareholders from Operations	**$ 110,514,629**

Table 13.3 PTP Statements of Changes in Net Assets

Statements of Changes in Net Assets		
For the Six Months Ended May 31, 2018 (Unaudited) and the Year Ended November 30, 2017	*2018*	*2017*
Operations:		
Net investment income (loss), net of income taxes	$ 29,529,738	$(12,952,561)
Net realized gain, net of income taxes	9,433,244	88,577,321
Change in net unrealized appreciation (depreciation), net of income taxes	71,551,647	(153,326,985)
Increase (Decrease) in Net Assets Applicable to Common Shareholders from Operations	***110,514,629***	***(77,702,225)***
Distributions to Common Shareholders from (Note 1):		
Dividends	–	(83,933,473)
Return of capital	(49,935,739)	(15,639,641)
Decrease in Net Assets from Distributions to Common Shareholders	***(49,935,739)***	***(99,573,114)***
Fund Share Transactions:		
Reinvestment of distributions (165,870 and 169,574 shares issued, respectively)	2,348,719	2,558,871

Statements of Changes in Net Assets		
For the Six Months Ended May 31, 2018 (Unaudited) and the Year Ended November 30, 2017	*2018*	*2017*
Increase in Net Assets from Fund Share Transactions	***2,348,719***	***2,558,871***
Increase (Decrease) in Net Assets Applicable to Common Shareholders	***62,927,609***	***(174,716,468)***
Net Assets Applicable to Common Shareholders:		
Beginning of period	973,538,089	1,148,254,557
End of Period*	**$ 1,036,465,698**	**$ 973,538,089**
*Includes accumulated net investment loss, net of income taxes:	$(99,455,331)	$(128,985,069)

Table 13.4 PTP Statement of Cash Flows

Statement of Cash Flows (Unaudited) *For the Six Months Ended May 31, 2018*	
Increase (Decrease) in Cash:	
Cash Provided (Used) by Operating Activities:	
Net increase in net assets applicable to common shareholders resulting from operations	$ 110,514,629
Adjustments to reconcile net increase in net assets resulting from operations to net cash provided (used) by operating activities:	
Purchases of portfolio securities	(65,532,464)
Sales of portfolio securities	54,174,496
Net purchases, sales and maturities of short-term investments	(6,592,938)
Return of capital	55,009,223
Decrease in dividends and distributions receivable	455,673
Decrease in prepaid expenses	33,412
Decrease in income tax receivable	1,337,502
Increase in interest receivable	(11,069)
Increase in investment management fee payable	65,689
Decrease in Directors' fees payable	(11,334)
Decrease in interest payable	(90,676)
Decrease in accrued expenses	(76,105)

Statement of Cash Flows (Unaudited) *For the Six Months Ended May 31, 2018*	
Decrease in distributions payable to Mandatory Redeemable Preferred Stockholders	(6,042)
Decrease in deferred tax liability	(46,321,890)
Net realized gain on investments	(12,560,886)
Change in net unrealized appreciation (depreciation) of investments	(61,049,056)
Net Cash Provided by Operating Activities*	***29,338,164***
Cash Flows from Financing Activities:	
Distributions paid on common stock	(47,587,020)
Proceeds from loan facility borrowings	59,000,000
Repayment of loan facility borrowings	(41,000,000)
Decrease in deferred debt issuance and offering costs	168,122
Decrease in preferred stock offering costs	80,734
Net Cash Used in Financing Activities	***(29,338,164)***
Cash at the Beginning of Period	–
Cash at the End of Period	–
Non-cash Financing Activities:	
Proceeds from reinvestment of distributions	$ 2,348,719

* Included in operating expenses is cash of $ 7,930,827 paid for interest and commitment fees on borrowings and $ 49,000 paid for income taxes, net of refunds, if any.

CHAPTER 14

Partnerships: Merger and Divisions

Under section 708(b)(2)(A), if two or more partnerships merge or consolidate, "the resulting partnership shall, for purposes of IRC section 708, be considered the continuation of any merging or consolidating partnership whose members own an interest of more than 50 percent in the capital and profits of the resulting partnership." Under Treasury Regulations section 1.708-1(c)(1) if the members of none of the merging partnerships collectively own more than 50% of the capital and profit interests of the resulting partnership, then all of the merging partnerships terminate. Section 708(b)(2)(B) provides that, in the case of a division of a partnership into two or more partnerships, the resulting partnerships (other than any resulting partnership the members of which had an interest of 50% or less in the capital and profits of the prior partnership) are considered a continuation of the prior partnership.

14.1 GENERAL

Under section 708(b)(2)(A), if two or more partnerships merge or consolidate, "the resulting partnership shall, for purposes of IRC section 708, be considered the continuation of any merging or consolidating partnership whose members own an interest of more than 50 percent in the capital and profits of the resulting partnership." Under Treasury Regulations section 1.708-1(c)(1) if the members of none of the merging partnerships collectively own more than 50% of the capital and profit interests of the resulting partnership, then all of the merging partnerships terminate. The resulting partnership is treated as a new partnership. The regulation further provides that if the merging partnerships are commonly owned, and the members of one partnership own more than 50% of the capital and profits of the resulting partnership, then the resulting partnership is generally treated as a continuation of that first partnership (with any other merging partnerships treated as terminating).

14.2 THE 50% THRESHOLD

The 50% threshold in the merger rules logically views a resulting partnership as a continuation only if one or more historic partners hold more than 50% of the partnership interests of the merging and resulting partnerships. Whether a partnership is old and cold (as opposed to newly formed) is not relevant. The merger rules also clearly establish that, if a resulting partnership is treated as a continuation of a merging partnership, then that merging partnership is treated as having terminated (even if it were in the process of dissolving and might otherwise be viewed as a continuing partnership under section 708(b)(1)). Finally, the merger rules also specify the types of partnership interests relevant to the overlap test: 50% of the capital and profit interests.

14.3 FORM OF A MERGER OR CONSOLIDATION

The two types of partnership mergers recognized by the IRS are assets-over form and assets-up form.

Assets-Over Form

A partnership merger is treated as an "assets-over" transfer, unless specifically structured as "assets-up." A partnership can transfer all its assets to another partnership in exchange for interests in that partnership, and immediately thereafter, the terminated partnership distributes interests in the resulting partnership to its partners in liquidation of the terminated partnership. This form of merger is called "assets-over," because the dissolving partnership's assets are conveyed over to the resulting partnership. In an assets-over merger, the terminating partnership contributes all assets and liabilities directly to the remaining partnership. In return, the remaining partnership distributes ownership to the terminating partnership which immediately distributes this ownership to its partners. Upon distributing this ownership in the remaining entity to the partners, the terminating partnership no longer retains any assets, liabilities, or equity and ceases to exist. In this type of merger, the basis of these items are unchanged and no gain or loss is recognized on the merger. The resulting basis for each partner will be equal to their basis before the merger plus or minus any adjustments resulting from a change in liabilities.

Assets-Up Form

The partnership can liquidate by distributing all its assets to its partners. They then contribute the assets to the resulting partnership. This form of merger is called "assets-up," because assets are transferred "up" to the partners. In an assets-up merger, the terminating partnership distributes all assets and liabilities to its partners who then contribute these items to the remaining entity in exchange for ownership. Despite the partners' transitory ownership of the terminated partnership's assets, the form of a partnership merger or consolidation will be respected for Federal income tax purposes if the merged or consolidated partnership that is considered terminated distributes all of its assets to its partners in liquidation of the partners' interests in the terminated partnership, and immediately thereafter, the partners in the terminated partnership contribute the distributed assets to the resulting partnership in exchange for interests in the resulting partnership. Furthermore, for the IRS to determine that an assets-up merger has occurred, the partnership must take all steps to attest that the assets have been legally transferred to the partners before being transferred to the surviving partnership. In certain situations, an assets-up merger allows partners to distribute assets in such a way to avoid or minimize gain recognition and produce a significant beneficial future tax result.

14.4 TAX CONSEQUENCES OF THE TERMINATED PARTNERSHIP

The partnership that is deemed to terminate for tax purposes under the partnership-merger rules is treated as follows:

- The terminated partnership is deemed to contribute its assets and liabilities to the continuing partnership in exchange for interests in the continuing partnership. In general, there is no gain or loss on the contribution.
- The terminated partnership receives a capital account credit based on the amount of money contributed and the FMV of property contributed, net of any liabilities.
- The terminated partnership's basis in the contributed assets carries over to the basis in the interests of the continuing partnership that it receives.
- The terminated partnership's holding period in the contributed assets tacks on to the holding period in the partnership interest received. Finally, it is worthy to note that the dissolved partnership's tax year terminates on the date of the merger.

14.5 TAX CONSEQUENCES OF THE CONTINUING PARTNERSHIP

The partnership that is deemed to continue for tax purposes under the partnership-merger rules is treated as follows:

- The continuing partnership generally has no gain or loss.
- The continuing partnership takes a carryover basis in the assets of the dissolved partnership.
- The holding period of the assets of the dissolved partnership "tacks." That is, the continuing partnership acquires whatever holding period the dissolved partnership had.
- The continuing partnership will generally step into the terminated partnership's shoes for depreciation and cost recovery of contributed assets of the dissolved partnership.

- The terminated partnership's contributions of unrealized receivables, inventory, and built-in capital loss property will retain their character in the continuing partnership.
- The continuing partnership's tax year does not close.

The federal income tax return for the year of the merger must state that the partnership is a continuation of the merging partnership. The continuing partnership must retain the same employer identification number.

14.6 TAX CONSEQUENCES TO THE PARTNERS

- The partners in a partnership merger do not recognize gain or loss on the transaction. Rev. Rul. 68-289, 1968-1 C.B. 314 provides that the partners in the non-continuing partnership are treated as contributing all of their assets and liabilities to the continuing partnership, in exchange for an interest in the continuing partnership.
- A partner may, however, recognize gain or loss in certain instances. This usually occurs if the partner's net share of liabilities allocated to the partner is reduced so there is a deemed cash distribution that triggers taxable gain.
- The partners of the terminated partnership step into the dissolved partnership's shoes with respect to their shares of capital accounts.
- The partners of the terminated partnership generally will have the same adjusted basis in the continuing partnership that they had in the terminated partnership.
- The continuing partnership may have a Code section 754 election (also known as a step-up in basis) in effect. If so, the partners of the terminated partnership may receive a special basis adjustment in the assets of the continuing partnership. This adjustment extends as far as a partner's basis in continuing partnership interests received differs from his basis in the continuing partnership's assets.

14.7 PARTNERSHIP DIVISIONS

The IRC neither defines what constitutes a partnership division nor prescribes a form for a partnership division. However, section 708(b)(2)(B) provides that, in the case of a division of a partnership into two or more partnerships, the resulting partnerships (other than any resulting partnership the members of which had an interest of 50% or less in the capital and profits of the prior partnership) are considered a continuation of the prior partnership. Section 1.708-1(b)(2)(ii) provides that any other resulting partnership is not considered a continuation of the prior partnership but is considered a new partnership. If the members of none of the resulting partnerships owned an interest of more than 50% in the capital and profits of the prior partnership, the prior partnership is terminated.

14.7.1 Types of Partnership Divisions

The IRS regulations provide that the form of a partnership merger or division accomplished under laws of the applicable jurisdiction will be respected if the partnership undertakes the steps of either the Assets-Over Form or the Assets-Up Form.

The Assets-Over Form

In a partnership division under the "assets-over" form where at least one resulting partnership is a continuation of the prior partnership, the divided partnership contributes certain assets and liabilities to a recipient partnership or recipient partnerships in exchange for interests in such recipient partnership or partnerships, and immediately thereafter, the divided partnership distributes the interests in such recipient partnership or partnerships to some or all of its partners in partial or complete liquidation of the partners' interests in the divided partnership. However, in a division under the assets-over form where none of the resulting partnerships is a continuation of the prior partnership, the prior partnership will be treated as contributing all of its assets and liabilities to new resulting partnerships in exchange for interests in the resulting partnerships; and, immediately thereafter, the prior partnership will be treated as liquidating by distributing the interests in the new resulting partnerships to the prior partnership's partners.

The Assets-Up Form

(a) Assets-up form where the partnership distributing assets is a continuation of the prior partnership. Despite the partners' transitory ownership of some of the prior partnership's assets, the form of a partnership division will be respected for federal income tax purposes if the divided partnership (which must be a continuing partnership) distributes certain assets (in a manner that causes the partners to be treated, under the laws of the applicable jurisdiction, as the owners of such assets) to some or all of its partners in partial or complete liquidation of the partners' interests in the divided partnership, and immediately thereafter, such partners contribute the distributed assets to a recipient partnership or partnership's designated partners.
(b) Assets-up form where none of the resulting partnerships are a continuation of the prior partnership. If none of the resulting partnerships are a continuation of the prior partnership, then despite the partners' transitory ownership of some or all of the prior partnership's assets, the form of a partnership division will be respected for federal income tax purposes if the prior partnership distributes certain assets (in a manner that causes the partners to be treated, under the laws of the applicable jurisdiction, as the owners of such assets) to some or all of its partners in partial or complete liquidation of the partners' interests in the prior partnership, and immediately thereafter, such partners contribute the distributed assets to a resulting partnership or partnerships in exchange for interests in such resulting partnership or partnerships.

CHAPTER 15

Centralized Partnership Audit Regime

Under Section 6223 and the recently issued final regulations (T.D. 9839), partnerships are required to designate a partnership representative. Under the centralized partnership audit regime, the partnership representative has the sole authority to act on behalf of the partnership. The designated partnership representative is a partner or other person with substantial presence in the United States. The new regime replaces the consolidated audit proceedings under TEFRA and the electing large partnership provisions. A partnership can elect out of the centralized partnership audit regime for a tax year if the partnership is an eligible partnership that year. A partnership is an eligible partnership for a tax year if it has a hundred or fewer eligible partners.

15.1 GENERAL

The BBA created a new CPA regime effective for partnership tax years beginning after 2017. The new regime replaces the consolidated audit proceedings under Tax Equity and Fiscal Responsibility Act of 1982 (TEFRA) and the electing large partnership provisions. The new audit regime applies to all partnerships unless the partnership is an eligible partnership and elects out by making a valid election.

15.2 ROLE OF PARTNERSHIP REPRESENTATIVE

Under section 6223 and the recently issued final regulations (T.D. 9839), partnerships are required to designate a partnership representative (PR). Under the CPA regime, the PR has the sole authority to act on behalf of the partnership. The designated PR is a partner or other person with substantial presence in the United States. If the designated PR is an entity, the partnership must also appoint a designated individual (DI) to act on behalf of the entity partnership representative (EPR). The partnership must include information regarding the PR and DI (if applicable) on Form 1065. Additionally, the law grants the IRS the authority to designate a PR on the partnership's behalf where necessary. The IRS may designate a PR if it determines that a designation is not in effect under Regulations section 301.6223-1(f)(2).[41]

15.3 ELECTION OF PR

A partnership designates any person, an entity or itself as a PR, but they are required to have a substantial presence in the United States. If an entity is designated as a PR, the partnership must also appoint a DI to act on the entity's behalf. The DI must also have a substantial presence in the U.S.

For a PR or DI to have substantial presence in the United States, all the following must be true:

- The entity/individual has a U.S. taxpayer identification number (TIN).
- The entity/individual has a U.S. street address and a telephone number with a U.S. area code.
- The PR or DI acting on behalf of an EPR makes themselves available to meet in person with the IRS in the United States at a reasonable time and place as determined by the IRS in accordance with Treasury Regulation § 301.7605-1.

The partnership designates a PR separately for each tax year, and the designation is effective only for the tax year for which it is made [F.N: Regulations section 301.6223-1(c)(1)].

Example

A partnership designates *X* as the PR for the tax year ended December 31, 2018, but then, after a falling out with *X*, the partnership designates *Y* as the PR for the tax year ended December 31, 2019. In 2021, the IRS examines the partnership's 2018 tax return. *X* is the PR for the 2018 tax year, notwithstanding the fact that the partnership designated *Y* in 2019.

15.3.1 Actions of the PR

The actions of the PR on behalf of the partnership and the partners under subchapter C of Chapter 63 of the IRC include but are not limited to:

- Entering into a settlement agreement.
- Agreeing to a notice of final partnership adjustment (FPA).
- Requesting modification of an imputed underpayment (IU).
- Extending the modification period by agreement.

41. *See: Designation of the partnership representative by the IRS.*

- Waiving the modification period.
- Agreeing to adjustments and waiving the FPA.
- Extending the statutory periods for making adjustments by agreement.
- Making a push-out election.

15.3.2 Resignation and Revocation of the PR

Resignation by the PR: Under the final regulations, a PR or DI may resign for any reason by notifying the IRS in writing, only after the IRS issues a Notice of Administrative Proceeding (NAP). A PR or DI may not, unlike under the proposed regulations, pick his or her successor. The final regulations also require the IRS to provide written notice of the resignation to the partnership. Nevertheless, the IRS' failure to notify the partnership within 30 days of the PR's or DI's resignation does not affect the resignation, so long as the PR or DI resigned in accordance with the regulations and other guidance.

Revocation of the PR's designation: The partnership may revoke the designation of a PR or DI, for any reason, by notifying the IRS in writing[42] (Regulations section 301.6223-1(e)). The partnership may revoke a PR designation for a tax year for any reason by notifying the PR and the IRS in accordance with applicable forms and instructions, but the partnership must designate a successor PR. Revocation of a PR (entity or individual PR) requires the partnership to immediately designate a successor PR (entity or individual). If a successor EPR is made, the simultaneous appointment of a DI is also required. However, the flexibility for revoking a PR designation is limited where the PR has been designated by the IRS.

Designation by the IRS: If the IRS determines that a designation of a PR is not in effect, it has broad authority to designate a PR or DI for the partnership. Some circumstances under which the IRS can determine that no PR designation exists include:

- No substantial presence in the United States.
- The partnership failed to appoint a DI if the PR is an EPR.
- The partnership failed to make a valid designation of a PR.
- There was a valid resignation of PR or DI but no subsequent designation by the partnership.
- There are multiple revocations within the 90-day period and the IRS.
- There is no designation in effect.
- The PR is no longer in effect for any other reason as determined by other published guidance.

42. Regs. sec. 301.6223-1(e).

15.4 ELECTING OUT OF THE CPA REGIME

A partnership can elect out of the CPA regime for a tax year if the partnership is an eligible partnership that year. A partnership is an eligible partnership for a tax year if it has 100 or fewer eligible partners. A partner is an eligible partner if it is an individual, C corporation, foreign entity that would be treated as a C corporation if it was domestic, S corporation, or an estate of a deceased partner. The determination as to whether the partnership has 100 or fewer partners is made by adding the number of Schedules K-1 required to be issued by the partnership to the number of Schedules K-1 required to be issued by any partner that is an S corporation to its shareholders for the tax year of the S corporation ending with or within the partnership tax year. A partnership is not an eligible partnership if it is required to issue a Schedule K-1 to any of the following partners:

- A partnership.
- A trust.
- A foreign entity that would not be treated as a C corporation were it a domestic entity.
- A disregarded entity described in Regulations section 301.7701-2(c)(2)(i).
- An estate of an individual other than a deceased partner.
- Any person that holds an interest in the partnership on behalf of another person.

An annual election out of the CPA regime must be made on the eligible partnership's timely filed return, including extensions, for the tax year to which the election applies. The election is made by including the following information on Schedule B-2 (Form 1065) and filing with the tax return:

- The name of each partner.
- The TIN of each partner.
- The federal tax classification for each partner.
- If an S corporation is a partner, provide the names, TINs, and federal tax classification of any shareholder of the S corporation for the tax year of the S corporation ending with or within the partnership's tax year.

The election is annual, and once made annual may not be revoked without the consent of the IRS. A partnership that elects out of the CPA regime must notify each of its partners of the election within 30 days of making the election. By making the election out of the CPA regime, the partnership is asserting that all of the partners in the partnership meet the eligibility requirements under section 6221(b)(1)(C) of the IRC and you have provided all of the required information with the Form 1065.

15.5 ADMINISTRATIVE ADJUSTMENT REQUEST

A partnership may file an AAR under section 6227 with respect to any PRI and correct errors on a previously filed partnership return. However, a partnership may not file an

AAR solely for the purpose of changing the designation of a PR. The filing of an AAR will extend the section 6235(a)(1) statute date which is three years from the date the AAR was filed. A partnership may not file an AAR more than three years after the later of the date the partnership return for such taxable year was filed or the last day for filing such partnership return (without regard to extension); or after a NAP has been issued with respect to such taxable year. In such a case, the partnership must determine whether the adjustments requested in the AAR result in an IU. If so, the partnership must take the adjustments into account and make payment unless the partnership makes a valid election for the adjustments to be taken into account by the reviewed-year partners. Put differently, the partnership that files an AAR must calculate whether the requested adjustments result in an IU. If there is an IU, a partnership must either:

- make a payment on adjustments that result in an IU and push out adjustments that do not result in an IU to the reviewed-year partners; or
- push out all adjustments to the reviewed-year partners by making an AAR push-out election.

15.5.1 Period of Adjustment

A Period of Adjustment is the statute of limitation for making a partnership adjustment (not an assessment statute). The partnership adjustment must be made before the later of the date (1), (2) or (3) below:

(1) the last date to issue Notice of Proposed Partnership Adjustment (NOPPA), which is three years after the latest of:
    (a) the date the partnership return was filed;
    (b) the return due date; or
    (c) the date the partnership filed an AAR.
(2) if modification is requested in response to the NOPPA, the last date to submit a modification request plus the evaluation period (at least 270 days), and any extension of time for submission of the modification request; or
(3) if modification is not requested in response to the NOPPA, 330 days after issuance of the NOPPA (plus any extension of time for submission of the modification request).

15.6 PARTNERSHIP AUDIT

A partnership audit will begin with the IRS sending a NAP. Following this notice, the IRS will work with the PR to set a schedule for Information Document Requests requests and partnership responses. Unlike under TEFRA, under the CPA regime, partners are not entitled to notice regarding the start of an audit or any developments throughout the audit or appeals processes. The IRS will generally inform the PR of transactions or issues identified during audit that will be included in the NOPPA. The limitations period for issuance of the NOPPA is generally three years after filing of the partnership return, but may be extended. The proposed regulations confirm that partnerships may challenge proposed IUs in the IRS Office of Appeals but do not establish the procedures for transferring the case to appeals.

Managing the audit and, if necessary, the appeals process will be a key function of the PR. The proposed regulations are silent as to whether a PR may delegate day-to-day management of an audit. The NOPPA will identify any "IU," which is the additional tax liability resulting from a proposed partnership adjustment for any taxable year ("reviewed year") that must be paid by the partnership. The concept of an IU that may be collected directly from the partnership is one of the ways that the CPA regime seeks to avoid the difficulties in collecting the tax due under TEFRA

15.6.1 Notice of Administrative Proceeding

In general, the IRS mails to the partnership and PR a NAP when initiating an examination of the partnership for a taxable year, including an examination following an AAR filed by the partnership. A NAP is issued no earlier than 30 days but no later than 60 days from the issuance of the letter. Partnerships subject to the CPA regime and filing an AAR that result in an IU and any interest or penalties related to the IU should report the IU and any related interest and penalties on Form 1065 or 1065X (as applicable).

Section 6225(c) of the IRC allows a BBA partnership under examination to request specific types of modifications of any IU proposed by the IRS. One type of modification (under section 6225(c)(2) of the IRC) that may be requested is when one or more (reviewed year) partners file amended returns for the tax years of the partners which include the end of the reviewed year of the BBA partnership under examination and for any tax year with respect to which tax attributes are affected. *See* the Instructions for Form 8980.

15.6.2 Notice of Proposed Partnership Adjustment

A NOPPA is required to be issued to a partnership (Letter 5892) and the PR (Letter 5892-A) when the IRS is proposing adjustments to a partnership tax year. The NOPPA is issued after any appeals consideration of the substantive adjustments. The NOPPA provides that the PR may request modification of the computation of the IU and starts the period to request modification. The IRS must issue a NOPPA to the partnership and the PR by certified mail. The mailing of the NOPPA to the partnership and PR starts the 270-day window for the PR to submit a request to modify any IU amount reflected on the NOPPA. The timely issuance of the NOPPA is vital to protecting the statute of BBA cases. The NOPPA may not be mailed more than three years after the later of:

(1) the date on which the partnership return for the taxable year was filed;
(2) the return due date for the taxable year; or

(3) the date on which the partnership filed an AAR with respect to the taxable year.

15.7 AMENDED RETURN

Rather than filing an amended return, a partnership that is subject to the CPA regime must file either Form 8082, Notice of Inconsistent Treatment or AAR, or Form 1065X, Amended Return or AAR to request an administrative adjustment for an amount of one or more partnership-related items. Form 8082 must be used if filing electronically.

CHAPTER 16

Partnership Bankruptcy

As any other business entity, a partnership can file for bankruptcy protection under the laws. The major advantage of filing for bankruptcy is the automatic stay or halt against creditor's action to foreclose or collect debts during the bankruptcy proceeding. This stay protects the debtor partnership against harassment by creditors and gives the partnership time to reorganize or liquidate the business and develop a plan of debt settlement that is fairest to all creditors. The most serious disadvantage of bankruptcy is a loss of control by management. In Chapter 7 Liquidation, management loses control to a trustee. Since the trustee's purpose is to liquidate the partnership, this may not be a critical issue. In Chapter 11 Reorganization, even though the debtor partnership's management typically remains in place as a debtor in possession, some operating control is lost. For instance, the court must approve administrative expenses and actions outside the normal course of business, such as asset sales.

16.1 GENERAL

Article I, section 8, of the United States Constitution authorizes Congress to enact "uniform Laws on the subject of Bankruptcies." Under this grant of authority, Congress enacted the "Bankruptcy Code" in 1978. The Bankruptcy Code, which is codified as title 11 of the United States Code, has been amended several times since its enactment. It is the uniform federal law that governs all bankruptcy cases.

The procedural aspects of the bankruptcy process are governed by the Federal Rules of Bankruptcy Procedure (often called the "Bankruptcy Rules") and local rules of each bankruptcy court. There is a bankruptcy court for each judicial district in the United States. Each state has one or more districts. There are 90 bankruptcy districts across the United States. A fundamental goal of the federal bankruptcy laws enacted by Congress is to give debtors a financial "fresh start" from burdensome debts. This goal is accomplished through the bankruptcy discharge, which releases debtors from personal liability from specific debts and prohibits creditors from ever taking any action against the debtor to collect those debts. The Supreme Court made this point about the purpose of the bankruptcy law in a 1934 decision:

> [I]t gives to the honest but unfortunate debtor ... a new opportunity in life and a clear field for future effort, unhampered by the pressure and discouragement of preexisting debt.

16.2 TYPES OF BANKRUPTCY

Six basic types of bankruptcy cases are provided for under the Bankruptcy Code:

(1) Chapter 7 ("Liquidation"): contemplates an orderly, court-supervised procedure by which a trustee takes over the assets of the debtor's estate, reduces them to cash, and makes distributions to creditors, subject to the debtor's right to retain certain exempt property and the rights of secured creditors. Because there is usually little or no nonexempt property in most Chapter 7 cases, there may not be an actual liquidation of the debtor's assets. These cases are called "no-asset cases." A creditor holding an unsecured claim will get a distribution from the bankruptcy estate only if the case is an asset case and the creditor files a proof of claim with the bankruptcy court. In most Chapter 7 cases, if the debtor is an individual, he or she receives a discharge that releases him or her from personal liability for certain dischargeable debts. The debtor normally receives a discharge just a few months after the petition is filed.

(2) Chapter 9 ("Adjustment of Debts of a Municipality"): provides essentially for reorganization, much like a reorganization under Chapter 11. Only a "municipality" may file under Chapter 9, which includes cities and towns, as well as villages, counties, taxing districts, municipal utilities, and school districts.

(3) Chapter 11 ("Reorganization"): ordinarily is used by commercial enterprises that desire to continue operating a business and repay creditors concurrently through a court-approved plan of reorganization. The Chapter 11 debtor usually has the exclusive right to file a plan of reorganization for the first 120 days after it files the case and must provide creditors with a disclosure statement containing information adequate to enable creditors to evaluate the plan. The court ultimately approves (confirms) or disapproves the plan of reorganization. Under the confirmed plan, the debtor can reduce its debts by repaying a portion of its obligations and discharging others. The debtor can also terminate burdensome contracts and leases, recover assets, and rescale its operations in order to return to profitability. Under Chapter 11, the debtor normally goes through a period of consolidation and emerges with a reduced debt load and a reorganized business.

(4) Chapter 12 ("Adjustment of Debts of a Family Farmer or Fisherman with Regular Annual Income"): provides debt relief to family farmers and fishermen with regular income. The process under Chapter 12 is very similar to that of Chapter 13, under which the debtor proposes a plan to repay debts over a period of time—no more than three years unless the court approves a longer period, not exceeding five years. There is also a trustee in every Chapter 12 case whose duties are very similar to those of a Chapter 13 trustee. The Chapter 12 trustee's disbursement of payments to creditors under a confirmed plan parallels the procedure under Chapter 13. Chapter 12 allows a family farmer or fisherman to continue to operate the business while the plan is being carried out.

(5) Chapter 13 (" Adjustment of Debts of an Individual With Regular Income"): is designed for an individual debtor who has a regular source of income. Chapter 13 is often preferable to Chapter 7 because it enables the debtor to keep a valuable asset, such as a house, and because it allows the debtor to propose a "plan" to repay creditors over time—usually three to five years. Chapter 13 is also used by consumer debtors who do not qualify for Chapter 7 relief under the means test. At a confirmation hearing, the court either approves or disapproves the debtor's repayment plan, depending on whether it meets the Bankruptcy Code's requirements for confirmation. Chapter 13 is very different from Chapter 7 since the Chapter 13 debtor usually remains in possession of the property of the estate and makes payments to creditors, through the trustee, based on the debtor's anticipated income over the life of the plan. Unlike Chapter 7, the debtor does not receive an immediate discharge of debts. The debtor must complete the payments required under the plan before the discharge is received. The debtor is protected from lawsuits, garnishments, and other creditor actions while the plan is in effect.

(6) Chapter 15 ("Ancillary and Other Cross-Border Cases"): aims to provide an effective mechanism for dealing with cases of cross-border insolvency.

16.3 PARTNERSHIP AND BANKRUPTCY: THE PROS AND THE CONS

As any other business entities, a partnership can file for bankruptcy protection under the laws. The major advantage of filing for bankruptcy is the automatic stay or halt against creditor's action to foreclose or collect debts during the bankruptcy proceeding. This stay protects the debtor partnership against harassment by creditors and gives the partnership time to reorganize or liquidate the business and develop a plan of debt settlement that is fairest to all creditors. The automatic stay also protects creditors against other creditors' rush to collect debts first. However, this automatic stay does not necessarily protect the partners from legal action if, for example, they have guaranteed the partnership's debts. Another important advantage of bankruptcy to the debtor partnership is the avoidance powers it gives. With these powers, the partnership can reject unfavorable contracts and leases and overturn certain transactions deemed to have given an unfair preference to one creditor over other creditors. This maximizes the value of the debtor business to the creditors under the plan of reorganization or liquidation. However, bankruptcy filing does not only provide advantages, but it does come with some disadvantages as well. The most serious disadvantage of a bankruptcy proceeding is a loss of control by management. In Chapter 7 Liquidation, management loses control to a trustee. Since the trustee's purpose is to liquidate the partnership, this may not be a critical issue. In Chapter 11 Reorganization, even though the debtor partnership's management typically remains in place as a debtor in possession, some operating control is lost. For instance, the court must approve administrative expenses and actions outside the normal course of business, such as asset sales. Another disadvantage of a bankruptcy proceeding is that reporting requirements are more burdensome. Furthermore, a partnership in Chapter 11 is unlikely to react as quickly to the changing business environment due to the administrative requirements imposed by the bankruptcy and the general reluctance of most debtors in possession to take any risk. Other disadvantages include significantly higher legal and administrative costs, loss of customers because of the stigma attached to filing bankruptcy, and the physical and psychological toll on the partners and management resulting from a legal proceeding. Finally, and perhaps more importantly, it is common for one or more partners to personally guarantee the partnership's debt. If the debt is not paid off or arrangements are made to liquidate the debt in bankruptcy, the creditors will look to the partners' personal assets to satisfy the obligation. The partners may be left with a larger personal liability than if they had negotiated with the creditors themselves in an informal workout, and one or more may be forced into personal bankruptcy. Since partners often have no idea whether they have guaranteed one or more debts, it is worthwhile reviewing credit cards, line of credit, and other loan applications to determine whether any such guarantees exist.

16.4 BANKRUPTCY UNDER SUBCHAPTER K

IRC section 1399 provides: "Except in any case to which section 1398 applies, no separate taxable entity shall result from the commencement of a case under title 11 of the United States Code."

That is, under IRC section 1399, the filing of bankruptcy by a partnership does not create a separate taxable entity for federal income tax purposes. As a result, the partnership's tax attributes are unaffected by the bankruptcy filing; partnership income and loss continue to pass through to the partners under the usual partnership rules. In general, debt discharge income is recognized as partnership income and, thus, flows through to the partners. The debt discharge exceptions of section 108 are then applied at the individual partner level.

16.4.1 Partnership Dissolution

Under the Uniform Partner Partnership Act, the bankruptcy of a partner generally dissolves the general partnership. However, dissolution provisions often conflict with federal bankruptcy law principles. Moreover, disagreement does exist among the courts on whether dissolution provisions should be given any effect in bankruptcy.

16.4.2 Partnership Agreement and Bankruptcy

Until the enactment of the Bankruptcy Reform Act of 1978, unambiguous contractual *ipso facto* provisions such as section 7.5E were *enforceable* against Chapter 11 debtors, debtors in possession, and their estates. Congress reversed course in 1978, however, with its enactment of various Code provisions, which invalidate contractual *ipso facto* provisions for the reason that automatic termination of a debtor's contractual rights frequently hampers rehabilitation efforts by depriving the Chapter 11 estate of valuable property interests at the very time the debtor and the estate need them most. Some courts have likewise treated partnership agreements as executory contracts when the issue was not disputed. The term "executory contract" in the Bankruptcy Code refers to a contract in which performance remains due to some extent on both sides.

16.4.3 Cancellation of Partnership Debt

IRC section 61 defines gross income as "all income from whatever source derived." Section 61(a)(12) specifically provides that gross income includes income from the discharge of indebtedness. However, section 108(a)(1)(A) provides that gross income does not include cancellation of indebtedness income if the discharge occurs in a title 11 case. Cancellation of indebtedness income recognized at the partnership level must be allocated among the partners based on their respective ownership percentages under the general rules of sections 702(a) and 704(b). That is, the receipt of cancellation of debt (COD) income increases the partner's basis of his or her partnership interest under section 705. Under section 108(d)(6), the COD income exclusion and attribute reduction rules are applied exclusively at the partner level. Therefore, insolvent partners may exclude their allocable share of COD income in whole or in part, while solvent partners would be taxed on their allocable share of COD income despite the underlying level of insolvency of the partnership, unless another exclusion under section 108 applies. Section 108(d)(3) defines insolvency as the excess of liabilities over the FMV of assets, as determined immediately before the debt discharge and including the debt to be discharged. The amount excluded from income by reason of a debtor's insolvency cannot exceed the amount of the debtor's insolvency. The taxpayer has the burden of proof in meeting the definition of insolvency. In computing a taxpayer's insolvency, nonrecourse debt is treated as a liability to the extent of the FMV of the property securing the debt. Nonrecourse debt in excess of the property's FMV is treated as a liability only to the extent it is discharged.

16.4.4 Forgiveness of Nonrecourse Debt

When nonrecourse debt is forgiven in return for a transfer of the collateral, a debtor recognizes section 1001 gain equal to the adjusted issue price of the debt less than the adjusted basis of the property that secures the debt, but the transfer does not give rise to COD income. That is, a creditor's foreclosure on property purchased with nonrecourse debt is deemed a sale by the debtor partnership, and the resulting gain is allocated among the partners under section 704. Conversely, COD income may become due when nonrecourse debt is satisfied with an amount of cash less than the debt canceled, and the borrower retains the collateral, or when the principal amount of nonrecourse debt is reduced.

In Revenue Ruling 2012-14, the IRS concluded that discharged excess nonrecourse liabilities "should be associated with the partner who in the absence of the insolvency or other section 108 exclusion would be required to pay the tax liability arising from the discharge of that debt."

Example 1

- A debtor incurs a $ 1 million nonrecourse debt secured by a building having a $ 1 million FMV.
- The value of the building then depreciates to $ 800,000, and the lender agrees to reduce the nonrecourse debt to $ 825,000.
- The debtor has other assets with an aggregate FMV of $ 100,000.

Result

- The debtor realizes COD income of $ 175,000 that is excluded under section 108(a)(1)(B) to the extent of the debtor's insolvency. In determining the debtor's insolvency, the $ 1 million nonrecourse debt is treated as a "liability" to the extent of $ 975,000, i.e., the sum of (i) the collateral's FMV of $ 800,000 and (ii) the "excess" nonrecourse debt discharge of $ 175,000.
- Thus, the debtor is "insolvent" to the extent of the excess of liabilities ($ 975,000) over the FMV of its assets ($ 900,000). Because the debtor is "insolvent" to the extent of $ 75,000 immediately prior to the discharge, the debtor recognizes COD income of $ 100,000.

Example 2

Same facts as in Example 1, save that this time, it is a partner who had loaned nonrecourse to a partnership.

Note: The IRS has ruled that a partner that has loaned nonrecourse debt to a partnership should not be allocated a share of those liabilities for purposes of applying the insolvency exception. In the example above, if the debtor were a partnership, the partners would normally be allocated both the COD income and the discharged nonrecourse liabilities according to the partnership agreement, under section 704(b).

16.4.5 Forgiveness of Recourse Debt

When recourse debt is forgiven, a debtor recognizes COD income equal to the excess of the adjusted issue price of the debt over the property's FMV, and IRC section 1001 gain equal to the property's FMV less than its adjusted basis.

16.4.6 Tax Claims under IRC Section 507(a)(2)

Under 11 USC § 506(a), the IRS has a secured claim when:

- it has properly filed a pre-petition Notice of Federal Tax Lien (NFTL), and there is equity in the debtor's property to which the lien attaches; or
- it has a tax claim that is subject to setoff under 11 USC § 553.

The allowed amount of a secured claim will be determined after a valuation of the property. The balance, if any, of the IRS' claim is allowed as an unsecured claim and classified as either priority or general unsecured. All properties of the debtor must be valued in order to ascertain the value of the federal tax lien. For purposes of determining the IRS' secured claim, the federal tax lien attaches to the debtor's property that became estate property as of the commencement of the case, including property exempted under 11 USC § 522. The federal tax lien also attaches to property exempt from federal tax levy. Some of the debtor's property never becomes property of the estate and is excluded. The value of the excluded property is not used to calculate the amount of the IRS' secured claim.

Under 11 USC § 506(b), a creditor is oversecured when the value of secured collateral exceeds the amount of the debt owed to the creditor. An oversecured creditor is entitled to post-petition interest on the secured claim. The creditor is also allowed any reasonable fees, costs, or charges provided by an agreement or by state statute under which the claim arose. When IRS is oversecured, IRS is entitled to receive post-petition interest on an allowed and oversecured claim. However, it is not necessary to file a claim in bankruptcy to preserve a lien on the debtor's pre-petition assets that are not sold and distributed during the bankruptcy case. While receiving a discharge will prevent a creditor from enforcing a dischargeable debt against the debtor personally, the IRS may enforce its lien for dischargeable taxes against the debtor's exempt property if an NFTL was filed before the bankruptcy petition was filed. However, a lien for dischargeable taxes cannot be enforced against the after-acquired property of the debtor. Excluded property never becomes property of the bankruptcy estate. The statutory lien remains a claim against pre-petition property even after the bankruptcy discharge. Thus, the IRS can levy on abandoned or excluded property to collect dischargeable liabilities after the discharge.

Under 11 USC § 544, the trustee has the rights and powers of a judgment lien creditor. Accordingly, if an NFTL has not been filed prior to the institution of the bankruptcy case, the tax claims will be unsecured. The date the NFTL was filed should be clearly shown on the proof of claim. The trustee may not use 11 USC § 544 or 11 USC § 545(2) to prevail over NFTLs filed pre-petition for the types of property described in IRC § 6323(b), since the trustee is not a "purchaser."[43]

16.5 COURT CASES

16.5.1 Briarpark v. Commissioner

The Fifth Circuit held in Briarpark v. Commissioner that discharge of a portion of undersecured nonrecourse debt conditioned on a sale of the real property securing the debt results in gain from a disposition of property under section 61(a)(3) rather than COD income under section 61(a)(12).

The facts of the case can be summed up as follows:

- In 1981, Briarpark was organized as a Texas LP, and James C. Motley was a general partner.
- During FYs 1983 and 1984, the partnership acquired a 3-acre parcel of land at 2925 Briarpark Road, Houston, Texas and constructed a 12-story office building on it.
- On September 27, 1983, the partnership borrowed $ 21,600,000 from InterFirst Bank Houston, N.A. to finance the acquisition of the property and the construction of the building. Motley personally guaranteed the principal, interest, penalties and fees on the loan.
- By December 31, 1986, the outstanding principal and accrued interest due on the loan was $ 24,700,000.
- On May 28, 1987, the partnership and InterFirst modified and extended the original loan pursuant to a modified loan agreement. At the time, InterFirst estimated that the FMV of the property was approximately $ 17,000,000. The original loan was converted from a recourse to a nonrecourse obligation, and accrued but unpaid interest in the amount of $ 3,100,000 was capitalized.
- Motley's personal obligation under his guarantee was limited to $ 5,000,000. Also on May 28, 1987, Briarpark obtained a $ 1,500,000 loan for tenant improvements on a nonrecourse basis.
- By January 21, 1988, First Republic Bank Houston, N.A. became the successor in interest to InterFirst. The Federal Deposit Insurance Corporation, as receiver for First Republic, assigned the modified loan and the built-out loan to NCNB Texas National Bank.
- In March 1989, Briarpark submitted an application to NCNB seeking to modify the loans to allow a cash sale of the building. In the summer of 1988, at the

43. *In re Waiter*, 45 F.3d 1023 (6th Cir. 1995); *In re Berg*, 121 F.3d 535 (9th Cir. 1997).

suggestion of the bank, Motley placed the building on the market, and in March 1989, he brought to the bank several similar proposals for the sale of the property.

- At that time, the bank considered as available options: (1) liquidation in the event of a default (but at that time there was no default); (2) refinancing (which was not an "easily obtained alternative at the level of the debt"); and (3) a sale/settlement, the loan officer expressing the view that "the bank will realize the highest value if the building is sold in 1989."
- In NCNB's view, the best proposal was a $ 12,700,000 cash sale offer.
- As of July 1989, Briarpark was in default on the loans.
- On July 21, 1989, the partnership signed a sale agreement to sell the property to Dan Associates. The gross purchase price for the property was $ 12,200,000. Dan Associates conditioned the purchase of the property upon the partnership's arranging the satisfaction or removal of the encumbrances for consideration paid to NCNB not in excess of $ 11,490,000.
- On July 31, 1989, NCNB agreed to release its liens to allow the sale of the property to Dan Associates for $ 12,200,000, with the proceeds being assigned to NCNB.
- On October 5, 1989, Briarpark and Dan Associates amended the sale agreement, reducing the gross sale price to $ 11,600,000. Under the amended agreement, Briarpark was required to arrange for the satisfaction of the loans and removal of the encumbrances for consideration not exceeding $ 11,036,000 plus a $ 175,000 payment by Motley in settlement of his guarantee.
- On October 11, 1989, Motley's liabilities exceeded his assets by $ 13,497,675. On October 16, 1989, NCNB agreed to allow the cash sale of the property for $ 11,600,000 and to settle with Motley on his guarantee for $ 175,000.
- On November 3, 1989, Briarpark, Motley, Dan Associates, and NCNB entered into a conditional release agreement. NCNB agreed to release the property from all liens and security interests upon satisfaction of the following conditions: (1) the sale of the property to Dan Associates for a minimum gross sales price of $ 11,600,000; (2) the assignment of the greater of the net sale proceeds or $ 11,036,000 sale proceeds to the bank, to be applied against the partnership's cash notes; (3) the transfer of the partnership's cash reserves to the bank; and (4) Motley's payment of $ 175,000 to the bank.
- On December 27, 1989, the outstanding balances of the modified and the build-out loan were $ 24,562,763 and $ 1,019,418, respectively.
- Briarpark sold the property to Dan Associates for $ 11,600,000. Briarpark incurred selling expenses of $ 554,901. Dan Associates paid the net sales proceeds of $ 10,936,532 to NCNB. The adjusted basis of the property was $ 11,105,733.
- Also on December 27, 1989, NCNB released the liens against the property and released Motley from his guarantee of the modified loan, in return for his payment of $ 175,000 in cash. The partnership transferred its cash reserves of $ 177,495 to NCNB. As of December 31, 1989, Briarpark had no assets and ceased business operations.

- On its income tax return for 1989, Briarpark reported cancellation of indebtedness income for $ 14,468,154 as a result of the November 3, 1989, conditional release agreement.

The reported amount was calculated as follows:

- The partnership also reported a net loss on the sale of the property in the amount of $ 61,245.
- Upon audit, the Commissioner determined that the property incorrectly reported discharge of indebtedness income under I.R.C. § 61(a)(12) on its return.
- The Commissioner asserts that the partnership realized a gain from dealings in property under I.R.C. § 61(a)(3) because the amount of the discharged debt that had encumbered the property was includable in the amount realized.
- The IRS mailed to the partnership a Notice of Final Partnership Administrative Adjustment proposing adjustments to the partnership's return to reflect realized gain from the sale of $ 13,920,936, rather than the reported loss of $ 61,245 and to eliminate the reported cancellation of indebtedness income.
- The T.C. agreed with the Commissioner that the partnership had realized gains from dealings in property under I.R.C. § 61(a)(3) rather than discharge of indebtedness income under § 61(a)(12). The court noted that, for purposes of §§ 61(a)(3) and 1001(b), "the amount realized from a sale or other disposition of property includes the amount of liabilities from which the transferor is discharged as a result of the sale or disposition."
- The court found that the sale of the property and the assignment of sale proceeds and transfer of the partnership's cash reserves to NCNB "has the same practical effect as several other transactions which have been held to be a 'sale or exchange.' " According to the court, the transaction at issue "is the functional equivalent of a foreclosure, reconveyance in lieu of foreclosure, abandonment, or repossession" because "the mortgagor in each case is relieved of debt encumbering property and also is relieved of the obligation to pay taxes and assessments against the property."
- The court rejected the partnership's argument that NCNB should be regarded as having forgiven, independently of the sale, the excess of the $ 25,582,181 debt over the $ 11,114,027 in cash received. Thus, the court disagreed with the partnership's assertion that the amount realized on the sale of the property to Dan Associates was only $ 10,936,532, or less than the partnership's adjusted basis in the property. Far from being "two independent events," as the partnership argued, the court found the record to be "replete with evidence" that the sale and the loan discharges were the "result of a single transaction involving the sale of encumbered property."
- The court reasoned as follows:

> NCNB conditioned the discharge of the loans upon the sale of the property, and Dan Associates conditioned the purchase upon that discharge. At the end of the day, NCNB had proceeds from the sale, Dan Associates had the

> property, and Briarpark was relieved of the entire balance of the loans. In the foregoing context, the arrangements among NCNB, Dan Associates, and Briarpark embodied a single transaction to sell the property securing the loans.

- The question on appeal is whether the T.C. erred by holding that the partnership realized a gain from dealings in property in the amount of $ 14,407,520.72, rather than cancellation of indebtedness income in the amount of $ 14,468,154.
- The Circuit Court held that the T.C. properly found that the partnership's disposition of the property was conditioned upon the relief of its debt and was therefore the functional equivalent of a foreclosure sale.

16.5.2 Chiligiran v. Commissioner

In Chilingirian v. Commissioner, a debtor was relieved of personal liability on two mortgages in the amount of $ 170,000. The debtor quitclaimed the deed to one of the mortgage holders, who then assumed liability for the remaining mortgage. The Sixth Circuit affirmed the T.C.'s decision that the debtor recognized capital gain under section 1001 equal to the excess of the amount of the mortgages discharged on the foreclosure over its basis in the property. It is not clear whether the property's value equaled $ 170,000—the principal amount of the two recourse mortgages—because the FMV was neither disclosed nor discussed.

The key facts of the case were as follows:

- In 1972, the Chilingirians, together with two partners, purchased a building known as the Crocker Professional Center in Mount Clemens, Michigan.
- In 1974, the Chilingirians bought out their partners in the Crocker Center and became the sole owners of the building. At that time, the Chilingirians obtained new financing for the property in the form of two mortgage notes. The first mortgage was with Fort Wayne Mortgage Company in the amount of $ 110,000. The second mortgage, which was for $ 60,000, was junior to the first mortgage and was obtained from Frank and Eunice Giambrone and Louis and Rose Davis, their original partners in the Crocker Center.
- The Chilingirians were personally liable on each of the mortgage notes.
- The Chilingirians' initial basis in the Crocker Center was $ 147,800. As of June 1978, their adjusted basis in the Crocker Center had been reduced to $ 124,275.
- In June 1978, the Chilingirians lost their interest in the Crocker Center through a nonjudicial foreclosure. At that time, they were relieved of their personal liability on the two mortgage notes in the amount of $ 170,000.
- The Chilingirians divested themselves of their interest in the Crocker Center through transferring that interest by quitclaim deed to the holders of the second mortgage, who assumed liability for the first mortgage.

- On February 1, 1975, the Chilingirians, together with Charles and Joanne Schwarz, purchased an office building and surrounding land known as the Medical Arts Plaza in Muskegon, Michigan.
- The Chilingirians and the Schwarzes entered into a mortgage agreement with American Savings Association for $ 480,000. An additional $ 150,000 mortgage on the property was entered into between the seller, R.A. Miller Industries, and Schwarz Enterprises.
- On September 8, 1975, the Schwarzes gave a quitclaim deed for their interest in the Medical Arts Plaza to the Chilingirians in exchange for $ 2,500 and again the Chilingirians were fully liable on the recourse notes.
- In 1977, a judicial foreclosure was initiated by American Savings Association against the Medical Arts Plaza.
- The Chilingirians appealed the judgment of foreclosure to the Michigan Court of Appeals. Subsequently, there was a settlement. Under the terms of the settlement, the Chilingirians conveyed the Medical Arts Plaza by deed and paid an additional $ 10,000 to American Savings in exchange for relief from liability on the $ 480,000 mortgage note due to American Savings.
- Subsequent to these transactions, an Internal Revenue Agent conducted audits of two projects in which the Chilingirians were investors. The agent audited the Medical Arts Plaza for taxable years 1975 and 1976, and Courthouse Plaza, a third property, for taxable years 1976 and 1977. These audits were closed in January and March 1979, respectively.
- In October 1981, another Internal Revenue Agent began auditing the Chilingirians' tax returns for taxable years 1977 through 1980. This audit was closed by December 1982.
- The Chilingirians' tax returns for 1979 and 1980 had not been filed at the time the audit began and remained unfiled on May 14, 1984, when statutory notices of deficiency for 1978, 1979 and 1980 were mailed to the Chilingirians.
- The statutory notices of deficiency determined deficiencies for those years based on the inclusion of gains from the foreclosure sales of the Crocker Center and the Medical Arts Plaza, and also determined additions to their tax liability for negligence, late filing, and failure to pay estimated tax.
- The Chilingirians timely filed a petition in the T.C. contesting the Commissioner's determinations.
- On September 22, 1986, the T.C. held that the Chilingirians realized $ 170,000 on the nonjudicial foreclosure of the Crocker Center because they were relieved from personal liability on the two mortgage notes in the amount of $ 170,000. After subtracting their basis in the property of $ 124,275, the T.C. found that the Chilingirians realized a gain of $ 45,725.
- With regard to the foreclosure of the Medical Arts Plaza, the T.C. determined that the Chilingirians' original basis in the property was $ 632,500, the total amount of both outstanding mortgages plus the $ 2,500 payment for the quitclaim deed. The T.C. then held that the amount of gain realized by the

Chilingirians was the difference between the amount of the mortgages discharged on the foreclosure and the Chilingirians' basis in the property after depreciation, plus the $ 10,000 deficiency judgment paid to American Savings.

- The T.C. sustained the Commissioner's determination of additions to tax for late filing and failure to file under section 6651(a) of the IRC, for negligence under section 6653(a), and for failure to pay estimated tax under section 6654.
- The T.C. held that the Chilingirians had not shown that there was reasonable cause for their failure to timely file income tax returns for the years in issue. Similarly, the T.C. found that the Chilingirians' failure to include the relief of their indebtedness in the amount realized on the foreclosure sales was not due to reasonable cause, and thus held them liable for the addition to tax for negligence. The T.C. noted that Mr. Chilingirian was an attorney who dealt extensively with the IRS during the years in issue. Finally, the T.C. held that because none of the statutory exceptions had been shown to be applicable, an addition to tax was mandatory for failure to pay estimated tax.
- The Chilingirians appealed the T.C.'s decision.
- The Chilingirians' primary contention on appeal was that no gain should be recognized on the foreclosure of property where the owner of the property is personally liable on the mortgage and any equity in the property is lost.
- The Circuit Court held that the T.C. properly determined that the Chilingirians were required to recognize as gain the difference between the amount they realized, the total amount of the outstanding mortgages less than their adjusted basis in the property:

> Where depreciation deductions have been taken (as in this case) the reason for the rule is even more pronounced because it recognizes that such deductions are an economic benefit to the taxpayer. It is clear that the rationale for the rule does not depend on whether the outstanding loan is recourse or non-recourse.

Bibliography

Brian C. Spilker (2020): Taxation of Individuals and Business Entities, McGraw-Hills, Chapter 20, p. 15.

Cunningham, Laura and Noel (2000): The Logic of Subchapter K, West Academic.

GAO (September 2014), Large Partnerships: Report to Congressional Requesters, p. 5.

H.R. Rep. No. 1337, 83d Cong., 2d Sess., A236 (1954); S. Rep. No. 1622, 83d Cong., 2d Sess., 405 (1954).

Monte A. Jackal (2017): Summaries of Aggregate and Entity Authorities, Tax Notes.

Nellen and Karlinsky (1992), Section 1374 and the S Corporation (Fall 1992), Journal of S Corporation Taxation.

Glossary

Flow-Through or Pass-Through Entity: An entity that allocates income or losses to its taxable owners, who pay any taxes. Income taxes generally are not paid by the pass-through entities, which include partnerships, S corporations, trusts, and estates.

Taxable Partner: A partner who is the final recipient of pass-through income or loss allocations for which they owe taxes. Taxable partners include C corporations or individuals.

Direct Partner: A partner who has a direct interest in the partnership. A direct partner may be a taxable partner or a nontaxable partner.

Foreign Partnership: A foreign partnership is a partnership that is not created or organized in the United States or under the law of the United States or of any state. *See* Notice 2010-41 for information on when a domestic partnership will be classified as foreign.

General Partner: A general partner is a partner who is personally liable for partnership debts.

Indirect Partner: A person holding an interest in a partnership through one or more pass-through partners.

Flow-Through or Pass-Through Partner: A partner which is a flow-through or pass-through entity.

Limited Liability Company: It is an entity formed under state law by filing articles of organization as an LLC. Unlike a partnership, none of the members of an LLC is personally liable for its debts.

Limited Liability Partnership: A limited liability partnership (LLP) is formed under a state limited liability partnership law. Generally, a partner in an LLP is not personally liable for the debts of the LLP or any other partner, or is a partner liable for the acts or omissions of any other partner solely by reason of being a partner.

Limited Partner: A limited partner is a partner in a partnership formed under a state LP law, whose personal liability for partnership debts is limited to the amount of money or other property that the partner contributed or is required to contribute to the partnership. Some members of other entities, such as domestic or foreign business trusts or limited liability companies that are classified as partnerships, may be treated as limited partners for certain purposes.

Nonrecourse Loans: Nonrecourse loans are those liabilities of the partnership for which no partner or related person bears the EROL.

Partnership: A partnership is the relationship between two or more persons who join to carry on a trade or business, with each person contributing money, property, labor, or skill and each expecting to share in the profits and losses of the business whether or not a formal partnership agreement is made.

Partnership Agreement: It includes the original agreement and any modifications. The modifications must be agreed to by all partners or adopted in any other manner provided by the partnership agreement. The agreement or modifications can be oral or written.

Tax Matters Partner (TMP)

The TMP is the primary representative of the partnership in dealing with IRS as well as the partners. The TMP can be a general partner designated by the partnership or, if no TMP is designated, the general partner with largest profit interest. Under certain circumstances, IRS may select a partner to be the TMP.

The statute and regulations define a number of timelines at stages of the audit that IRS, the TMP, or partners should complete, such as sending out the notification at the beginning and conclusion of the audit.

Table of Cases

Index

www.ingramcontent.com/pod-product-compliance
Lightning Source LLC
Chambersburg PA
CBHW071332230926
51849CB00002B/374
9789403533834